LIVING
Joyfully
IN TROUBLED TIMES

FROM BESTSELLING AUTHOR
TONI SORENSON

Covenant Communications, Inc.

Printed in the United States of America
First Printing: January 2016

22 21 20 19 18 17 16   10 9 8 7 6 5 4 3 2 1

ISBN 978-1-68047-882-2

LIVING
Joyfully
IN
TROUBLED
TIMES

OTHER BOOKS AND AUDIO BOOKS
BY TONI SORENSON

Thanks to so many people who exemplify joy.
Sam, your faith in me is the reason this book exists.
Eli, you never have a bad day and
won't allow me to have one when we're together.
Thanks for being my bud, Bud.

I'm so deeply grateful for my readers.
You're what make all the work worthwhile.
I learn so much from you.

For John Sandstrom, a man who finds joy in every
journey. A man who has stepped in and stepped up
and because of that, our lives have forever changed.
You've taught me not to look for my self-worth in others.
That there's beauty in an ugly rock. That a rainstorm will
bring a rainbow. That Jesus is never far away.
My gratitude to you and Judy extends beyond words. Just
thinking about your smile makes me smile.

Dear Reader,

A PHYSICIAN HAPPENED BY A house where a decrepit old man sat hunched on the stoop, smoking. The man looked up and gave the doctor a grin.

"You look happy," the doctor said. "What's your secret?"

"Well," the man said, still smiling, "I smoke two packs of cigarettes a day, I use illicit drugs, I drink a fifth of whiskey and a bottle of wine every day. I eat all the chocolate I want, indulge in every vice that suits me, and I never ever exercise."

The medical man was stunned. "How old are you?"

The guy stopped smiling. "Twenty-two."

So much of the world thinks we find fulfillment and joy by pursuing our own interests, indulging in carnal pleasures, and acquiring material possessions. But joy is not something we can pursue. Even if we could pursue it, we could never catch it. Joy is a gift from God for a life lived full and well. He wants to give us that gift. But for so many of us, living a truly joyful life seems unobtainable.

Part of our mortal experience is to go through spans of time when we feel less than joyful. We all suffer days where we feel anxious and uncertain. No one gets out of this life without having to navigate through the darkness of sadness and even depression.

But we're not here on earth to stay sad. We're here to experience joy. How can we do that in a world that seethes with reasons to be sorrowful? Life is so darn tough. Very bad things really do happen to very good people. It all seems so unfair and inexplicable.

It's not.

Life, in the end, will all be made just and merciful. But for now, you and I are living in a fallen world where the plan is to challenge us, to test us, to strengthen us.

If there's a vague shadow cast over your life, if you can't quite figure out what's wrong, and you just don't manage the levels of elation your neighbors and Facebook friends post, there is joy available to you. If something horrific has happened to you that has thrown a cloud over your joy, you can break out of that darkness.

Jesus is fully and compassionately aware of what's going on in your life. He knows exactly where you hurt. He knows how hard you try. He knows the trials before you. He knows more than just your name. He knows your life—the hardships and harrows, the strong points and weaknesses, the people, the secrets. He knows it all. And He loves you with His all. That means your Savior wants you to be joyful in spite of everything and everyone who wants to steal your joy.

This little book is full of truths and ideas and reminders on how you can live joyfully in troubled times. It's going to give you hope where the world just gives you pressure. It will give you positive affirmations to eradicate the negative voices Satan shouts in your ear.

If anyone knows how terrifying and bleak this life can be, I do. But I also know that through the Atonement of Jesus Christ, we can be healed, not just later, but now—this very second, mending can begin. What we need are tools to get the work done—spiritual tools. Get the scriptures out and read this book side by side with the word of God. Take some time to meditate on life and where the cracks are that need to be filled. Did you know the ancient Japanese custom was to fill the cracks in a broken vessel with gold? That way the thing that was broken not only had its beauty restored, but it also became more valuable than ever before.

What a concept! After God fixes our brokenness, we become stronger and more attractive, and our value increases.

As I do in all the things I write, I want to testify of a Father in Heaven who loves His children with a love that is flawless and infinite. I want to testify that Jesus Christ is our Savior, personal and powerful. I want to testify to the truths that have rescued me from the deepest pits of hell, not because of anything I am or anything I have done but because the God I worship is good and does good things on behalf of His wounded and weak children.

We live in a glorious world. More joy abounds than we can imagine. We just have to know how and where to find it. My hope is that this book will aid you in that—that it will become a roadmap to joy.

Table of Contents

Chapter One
GOD WENT TO A GREAT DEAL OF EFFORT

"Let us make man in our image, after our likeness."
—Genesis 1:26

IMAGINE THAT YOUR GREAT-GREAT SECOND cousin's aunt Helen put you in her will. When she passed away, an account was automatically set up in your name, and now you are a millionaire. Only you've never heard of this generous relative, and the letter to inform you of the good news has been lost in the mail, so even though you're rich, you don't know it.

How many people in this world don't know they are children of God and heirs to His will (see Romans 8:17)? Knowing we are children of a loving, caring Father in Heaven is the basis for a joyful life. This knowledge is what brings us blissful awareness; it's what will pull us through the dark and sludgy trials and what will motivate and inspire us to accomplish marvelous feats.

Sadly, most of the world is unaware of spiritual identity or inheritance. But *you* are aware! So . . . are *you* happy? Is *your* life joyful? We're not talking a life void of struggles and trials and occasional pain; we're talking an overall existence of joy. It's your right to live such a life.

There's a traveling art exhibit of T-shirts making its way around our nation. People who have suffered abuse of any kind can have a free T-shirt and art supplies to write their story on the material. The shirts are then hung on a single shared clothesline. It's humbling and daunting to walk past thousands of shirts that tell survivors' stories and bear their feelings. They all tell of pain caused by the hand of cruelty. Many of them tell of suffering caused by someone close, someone with the responsibility to protect but who, instead, became a perpetrator. One shirt read, "You hurt me thirty years ago, but I still feel the pain." Another shirt said, "You once knocked me down, but I'm back on my feet!"

A recent global study found that children who were abused physically, emotionally, or sexually are at a much greater risk for depression. I could have saved those researchers millions of dollars and years of labor. *Of course* children who are hurt grow up to be more susceptible to pain. I think it's what allows us a greater measure of empathy. We know what it's like.

Children who grow up with stability, safety, and unblemished love tend to turn into confident, successful, joyful people.

That doesn't mean there's not enough joy to go around. There is. And the fact that a child comes from a secure, safe, loving home doesn't guarantee a happy, balanced adult. There are few guarantees in life, but here's one—joy is possible. Joy is even probable when we align ourselves with God. Joy is yours for the asking, knocking, and opening.

Heavenly Father and Jesus Christ (and a whole lot of others) have gone to a great deal of effort to make it possible for us to live joyful lives. First of all, this marvel of a planet was created to be our home, a place where we have the opportunity to gain all kinds of experiences. Next, our bodies of flesh and blood—in the likeness of God's glorified body—were created for our advancement and joy. Next, our first father and mother, Adam and Eve, paved the road for us to leave heaven and come to earth cloaked in mortality.

Because of their transgression in the garden, you and I and every other mortal born into this life became subject to both spiritual and physical death. Physical death occurs with the separation of body and spirit; spiritual death happens when the spirit is separated from the presence of God.

When this happened, the only goal Adam and Eve had was to reenter the presence of God. But they had both sinned, and not even someone who has committed just a single sin can enter God's presence (see Revelation 21:27). It's just not possible. So there were Adam and Eve, out in the lone and dreary world, aching to return to God's presence.

And there was our loving, wise Heavenly Father, separated from the children who gave His life its purpose. We never talk about the fact that this separation worked both ways, because maybe we take it for granted that God already had things worked out. But, oh, how He wanted to be reunited with His fallen children. He wanted them back so much He implemented His perfect provisional plan to have His Only Begotten, beloved Son atone for original and consequent sin. That means Christ's Atonement covers eating the forbidden fruit. That means His Atonement covers whatever sins you and I have committed. Jesus is the price that was paid for our safe return to God's presence.

A Redeemer had to break the bonds of death; a Resurrection had to be made possible for all mankind. I testify to you that Jesus of Nazareth is that Redeemer. Not only did He conquer physical death, but He also made joy possible when He conquered spiritual death. Because of Him, we can return as new creatures to an old heaven, a familiar place where progress never stops. A place where God waits to welcome us.

We can go home.

That's the same good news the angels brought on a chilly spring night to a group of startled shepherds on the hillsides of Bethlehem: "Joy to the world!"

Let's stop right here and address a little part of the plan that gets overlooked too often. Adam and Eve lived in a paradise where there was no suffering, sorrow, or pain, BUT they did not, *could* not experience joy. What would that be like—to have God plant a garden and then plant you in it, but you were unable to revel in its majesty and beauty? You couldn't even appreciate another's company because you had never known loneliness. You couldn't know beauty because you'd never seen ugly. You couldn't know ease because you'd never experienced hardship. You couldn't know one because you were unfamiliar with the other.

Imagine that you live in the desert, where sand and scorching wind blow all the time. Imagine that the only tree in sight is a cactus. Imagine that the only animal you hear sing is a distant coyote. Imagine now that you are transported to a tropical rain forest, where a thousand different kinds of leafy green trees drip sweet water, where the air is warm and moist and rainbows shimmer in the air as sunlight filters down from a blue sky. The music of a thousand songbirds swells in the air.

You can appreciate the difference because you understand opposites. You know one, so you can understand the other. Lehi's family experienced something similar to this. They went from the deserts of the Middle East to the tropics of the Americas. When Lehi was recounting their experience with his son Jacob about the things that matter most, he explained this concept with near perfection: "For it must needs be, that there is an opposition in all things. If not so, my firstborn in the wilderness, righteousness could not be brought to pass, neither wickedness, neither holiness nor misery, neither good nor bad. Wherefore, all things must needs be a compound in one; wherefore, if it should be one body it must needs remain as dead, having no life neither death, nor corruption nor incorruption, happiness nor misery, neither sense nor insensibility" (2 Nephi 2:11).

There's so much in that single verse that we could camp on, but for our quest, let's go back to the one thing Lehi compares twice: misery. First he contrasts holiness to misery. Next he contrasts happiness to misery. Could it be that holiness is happiness? Could it be that without misery, we could not recognize and savor happiness?

Adam and Eve, just like you and me, had a veil of forgetfulness placed over their memories of pre-earth life. Does that mean that when they walked and talked with God, it was an experience they could not fully appreciate because they had never before been separated from Him?

Only when Adam and Eve elected to eat of the tree of knowledge, the tree that contrasted good and evil, were they separated both physically and spiritually from God. Only when they fell did they recognize the consequence of their actions. Being separated from God *is* misery. It's the ultimate misery.

This all seems rather bleak until we realize it was part of a plan for us to be able to lead bounteous, joyful, meaningful lives. Only when our parents understood good from evil, right from wrong, sweet from bitter were they capable of choosing and able to be obedient. As they were obedient, they were entitled to the same blessings available to us: inspiration and revelation and emotion.

Only *out* of the garden were our parents able to progress. To learn. To procreate and experience the joys and sorrows of parenthood. It was all part of a perfect plan that allows choice without God's interference—a perfect plan Satan was just waiting to try to thwart.

Certain health and fitness circles share a joke about this:

> In the beginning God created the heavens and the Earth. And the Earth was without form, and void, and darkness was upon the face of the deep.
>
> And Satan said, "It doesn't get any better than this."
>
> And God said, "Let there be light," and there was light. And God said, "Let the Earth

bring forth grass, the herb yielding seed, and the fruit tree yielding fruit." And God saw that it was good.

And Satan said, "There goes the neighborhood."

And God said, "Let us make man in our image, after our likeness, and let them have dominion over the fish of the sea, and over the fowl of the air and over the cattle, and over all the Earth, and over every creeping thing that creepeth upon the Earth." And so God created man in His own image; male and female created He them. And God looked upon man and woman and saw that they were lean and fit.

And Satan said, "I know how I can get back in this game."

And God populated the earth with broccoli and cauliflower and spinach, green and yellow vegetables of all kinds so man and woman would live long and healthy lives.

And Satan created fast-food chains, and those chains brought forth the ninety-nine-cent double cheeseburger. And Satan said to man, "You want fries with that?"

Yes, indeed. Satan has a little something on the side that might look appetizing, but it doesn't come without a devastating price. He did his best to convince Adam and Eve that once they fell from grace, there was no grace available to them. I testify to you that is simply not true. God's grace is allotted just for sinners.

There Is No Secret to Happiness
The joke goes on and on . . . because whatever God creates, Satan counters. Satan is a miserable devil. He will always be miserable

because he chose the path of misery. While there will be times in our lives when misery is our company, we don't have to live in misery. We have options. Regardless of our circumstances, we can experience lasting joy by understanding God's plan and keeping His commandments. That takes work, understanding, and a whole lot of trial and error.

While the world searches for the secret to happiness, we know there is no secret. God has plainly revealed that the only way to be truly and lastingly happy is to keep the commandments. Don't groan or toss this book against the wall. It's glorious news, this obedience factor. Obedience is the magic key to happiness now and joy later. President Gordon B. Hinckley taught from the pulpit in the October 1971 general conference that our happiness, progress, prosperity, and ultimate exaltation depend on our obedience (see "If Ye Be Willing and Obedient," Conference Report, Oct. 1971).

Think of every commandment not as a fence to keep you in but as a barrier to keep harm out. His fence does not limit our agency; it expands it. That doesn't make a lot of worldly sense, but God's ways are not man's ways, and that's the way it works. His restrictions expand our agency and increase our borders.

When my mother was a young girl, she said, "I'm going to try smoking cigarettes because I'm free to do what I like."

After a week of smoking, she was no longer free to do what she liked. Her body craved nicotine. Her brain told her she had to smoke. Until the end of her life, cigarettes confined her, chained her, and stole her agency.

We're silly mortals, thinking rebellion is freedom when just the opposite is true. We're foolish because we believe the world's lie that God made commandants so He could control us. The commandments are in place to prove God's love for us, to help us find joy and a path back home to Him. As our loving Father, He made a way through His Beloved Son, Jesus, for this reason: "For behold, I . . . have suffered these things for all, that they might not suffer . . . even as I" (D&C 19:16–17).

The bottom line is that our Father in Heaven, through the hard work and design of Jesus Christ, went to a whole lot of effort to make our stay on earth both memorable and enjoyable. Why, then, are two-thirds of the world's population perpetually unhappy and lost? Even baptized, covenant-making members of the Church might fall prey to the following scenario:

Do you know your eternal identity?

Huh?

Do you realize your eternal worth?

Umm . . .

Do you know your individual eternal purpose?

Uh-uh.

We grow unhappy when we grow apart from our Father in Heaven. It's that simple and that complex. The connection between us is Jesus Christ; He is our connection to joy. That's all fine and dandy, but HOW do I manage a joyful life in a miserable world? Here are a few markers to consider:

Do you spend time doing what you truly love? Do you even know what it is you love most?

Are you working consistently on at least three concrete, doable goals?

Do you murmur?

Do you waste time? A lot of time?

Do you talk about people more than you talk about ideas?

Do you neglect your health—diet, exercise, and sleep?

When is the last time you created something beautiful and uniquely you?

How often do you go out of your way to help someone else in need?

Do you like the day-to-day pattern of your life?

Can you make a list of things that inspire you?

How often do you laugh out loud?

Are you in debt for things that don't contribute to the quality of your life?

Do you spend time with people who inspire you?

Do you travel outside your comfort zone on a regular basis?

Do you set aside time each and every day to spend alone with God?

How you answer these questions largely determines how you live your life. If you're in need of some adjustments, there are spiritual tools available. You just need to know where to find them and how to use them.

Be Aware

How many of us make a conscientious effort to be aware of God's goodness that abounds all around us? God wants you to be joyful. It's His divine desire to see you happy, successful, and living a joyful life even though the world around you is unhappy. That's how we should all live: like we have our Father's support and blessing to be joyful. To smile. To laugh. To live. Live! Live! Live!

To be joyful, we must be aware—aware that we are at war with Satan, who wants to steal our joy. He wants us to be miserable because he's miserable. God wants us to be happy because He's happy. So we must be aware that we are in a battle. Every day, sometimes many times a day, we must choose joy over misery.

Satan Is a Killjoy

Because Lord went to endless effort to ensure our joy, Satan will stop at nothing to steal it. "Wherefore, men are free according to the flesh; and all things are given them which are expedient unto man. And they are free to choose liberty and eternal life, through the great Mediator of all men, or to choose captivity and death, according to the captivity and power of the devil; for he seeketh that all men might be miserable like unto himself" (2 Nephi 2:27).

Let's break this down. First, to ensure our joy, God gave us freedom according to the flesh. That means with mortality came the ability to choose freely. It's the most precious gift we can possess and the only gift we can give back to God by choosing to honor and serve Him.

Read that scripture again. What does the word *expedient* even mean? It means suitable or efficient for accomplishing a purpose. That purpose, according to scripture, is to have joy. Joy comes from obedience and a closeness with God, something Satan does not—and will never—have.

If you return to the questions posed before, you can see how Satan would answer those questions. You can clearly see how miserable he must be.

On the other hand, we have a chance to be joyful no matter how miserable our circumstances.

Lessons from Lehi

Let's talk about joy in comparison to happiness. Author J. D. Salinger wrote, "The fact is always obvious much too late, but the most singular difference between happiness and joy is that happiness is a solid and joy a liquid" (from "De Daumier-Smith's Blue Period," *Nine Stories* [New York: Little, Brown, and Company, reprint edition, 1991]).

Happiness is temporary, but joy is lasting. Some philosophers propose that happiness is derived from external sources, while joy is born within.

All of those ideas are viable. The ultimate goal is joy. Everyone wants it, but not everyone understands what it really is and how to obtain it, keep it, and expand it.

The other day I watched my little grandchild run after a wet, soapy balloon. Every time her little hands grabbed it, it slipped free of her clutch—over and over and over until finally the balloon popped, and that was that. It made me think of how elusive our quest for joy can be. We run. We grab. We chase. We grip. And then we lose.

That's the devil's plan—to entice us with something we can't quite manage to grab and then take it from us after we've spent our resources chasing it.

That's not the Lord's plan. And a balloon is not the reward. Eternal life is the reward—to live in a place where and in a way in which progression is eternal, relationships continue and grow, and power and knowledge and stewardship have no end.

Latter-day Saints have a unique relationship with the word *joy* and the concept of it. The prophet Lehi explained it simply and best when he was teaching his son Jacob the most basic, meaningful principles of the gospel. We know it well. Even Primary children can quote, "Adam fell that men might be; and men are, that they might have joy" (2 Nephi 2:25).

Rewind.

What we often fail to realize is the context of the conversation between this aged father and his son. Lehi was once a wealthy businessman in Jerusalem. He was respected and revered as a Jewish leader. He had a faithful wife and sons and daughters. A comfortable home. A cushy life.

Lehi was willing to sacrifice all of it to honor his life's purpose, which was to preach the gospel to a sinful people. Once Lehi did that, his entire life changed. The lives of his wife and children changed—dramatically.

Then, years later, a wilderness behind them and a new life before them, Lehi spoke to Jacob, who never knew the comfort of Jerusalem. He was born a displaced person in the wilderness. He was born into a warring family, a divided unit where there was constant bickering among his siblings. He watched his mother and father suffer. He suffered. There wasn't any place to go to get away from the perpetual unhappiness of an unhappy family.

For those of us who have lived in an inharmonious family, we can imagine Jacob's upbringing. However, I wasn't raised in the wilderness with scalding temperatures, carpets of sand, and forever-blowing winds. Jacob was. I wasn't surrounded by snakes and robbers. Jacob was. I didn't have to hunt with my bow to find food. Jacob did. Add to all of that the fact that his parents were older, even elderly, and that because he loved all of his brothers, to see them divided had to be heartbreaking.

Lehi, in his final days, addresses Jacob as the son born "in the days of my tribulation in the wilderness." He acknowledges:

"In thy childhood thou hast suffered afflictions and much sorrow."

But then Lehi underscores what we all need to underscore if we are going to find joy in an unhappy world: "Nevertheless . . . thou knowest the greatness of God; and he shall consecrate thine afflictions for thy gain" (2 Nephi 2:2).

Nevertheless.

Afflictions for gain.

We know the greatness of God.

We know what the Lord told Joseph Smith when he was incarcerated in a jail constructed of wood and metal, mired in unspeakable filth: "Know thou, my son, that all these things shall give thee experience, and shall be for thy good" (D&C 122:7). These words were spoken during the coldest four and a half months of a Missouri winter. No blankets or quilts or even sheets were provided. Joseph and his companions were forced to sleep on a freezing stone floor with only a scant covering of straw. The food was scarce and of the most wretched quality. The jailers were vile men with vile mouths. They spoke words that were vicious and repugnant to Joseph. Yet it was here that Joseph received some of the most tender and powerful modern revelations.

Long before Joseph was incarcerated, the Lord allowed the Apostle Paul to suffer miserably in jail. From a dark and dank prison, Paul wrote: "Rejoice in the Lord alway: and again I say, Rejoice" (Philippians 4:4). He was writing to express his heartfelt appreciation and affection to the believers who offered their material support to him and the ministry. "I thank my God upon every remembrance of you, always in every prayer of mine for you all making request with joy, for your fellowship in the gospel from the first day until now" (Philippians 1:3–5).

His heart overflowed with gratitude while he was near the end of his Roman imprisonment. The Philippians were worried about the sufferings their beloved leader was enduring. Historians agree that at the time of this writing, Paul was standing in the center of the city sewer, up to his thighs in human waste. If Paul could say "Rejoice" in that place and under those circumstances, we can say it from our homes and workplaces and schools and just about anywhere.

A desert.

A jail.

A sewer.

Circumstances don't determine our joy. *We* determine our joy. How? By what we think about and what we prioritize.

Let's stop again and make one thing clarion clear. People (like me) who suffer clinical depression are not expected to magically change their thoughts and their lives. Chemical imbalance makes joy even more elusive than usual, but we believe in a God whose very presence angels announced with tidings of great joy. We believe in a God who has gone to a whole lot of trouble to make *His* joy available to us. We believe in a God who has given us bodies and an earth, who has surrounded us with light, truth, and opportunity, the agency to choose, and a promise that He will be there when we call out to Him.

I'm not saying clinical depression can be cured by prayer alone. But I'm also not saying it can't be. What I am saying is that God will guide us to the answers we need if we seek Him and the inspiration of His Holy Spirit.

The Best News Ever

This is glorious news. The best news ever. Jesus wants us to have joy: "These things have I spoken unto you, that my joy might remain in you, and that your joy might be full" (John 15:11).

Our faith teaches us that God wants ALL of His children to live joyfully—emphasis on FULLY. On that point alone, I would convert to Mormonism. It is life-changing news that God loves ALL of His children and desires that ALL of us be joyful. That we live to our highest potential. We believe God wants us to be happy! That's a pretty drastic difference from the masses who believe God takes pleasure in our suffering, that He delights in punishing us, and that He waits for us to commit a sin that will exclude us from His presence for eternity.

One afternoon I found myself lost in the Church of the Holy Sepulcher in Jerusalem. All of the wailing, incense smoke, and darkness got to me. I wandered down one corridor and then another until I came to the end of what looked like an abandoned, soot-stained stone hallway. Looking up, I saw a massive painting of Christ. It appeared ancient and unkempt. The paint had cracked in places; the edges of the work were peeled back and floppy. And the man depicted was a horrifying and unfamiliar depiction of Christ with a scepter, a whip, and a globe of the world.

It was a heartbreaking experience for me. This was not the Jesus I had come to know. There was no mercy in the man—only keen punishment. Everything about the depiction was dark, terrifying, and sad.

It was not a portrait of the loving, merciful, joyous God who had come readily to my rescue. It was not the God I worshipped. The man in the painting was a Christ who delighted in our mortal agony.

We know better. Our motto can be summed up in the Apostle Paul's declaration to the Romans that nothing "shall be able to separate us from the love of God, which is in Christ Jesus our Lord" (Romans 8:39).

The God we know and love loves us. Knows us. Cares about our well-being and the level of our joy. For starters, He gave us life. He created bodies that are capable of touching, tasting, seeing, hearing, and smelling. Shame on us for taking our miraculous bodies for granted—or worse, for neglecting or abusing them.

How many different textures has the Lord created for us to touch? How many foods and spices and flavors can the human tongue taste? Is there a limit to the beauty the eye can behold? Could you list all of the sounds you hear in a single day? How about during the duration of a lifetime? And smells—the subtle and the pungent—they are all for your benefit. To bring you joy.

In certain sacred settings within the gospel context, we learn that we worship a God who adores variety. He loves brazen hues and bold designs. He cherishes the soft and small and muted too. His creations know no limits. And the pinnacle of all of His creations is the person you see in the mirror. Bet you didn't know God's favorite color is purple. Don't believe me? Study the building of Solomon's temple.

What's your favorite color? Taste? Sight? Smell? Texture?

To remind us that we are God's beloved children and that we live in a world that continually testifies of His love for us, Elder Richard G. Scott once asked the members of the Church how long it had been since they'd taken time to watch a sunset (see "Finding Joy in Life," Conference Report, April 1996). I made a challenge out of the question, and when I found myself in the Gulf of Mexico, alone and with camera in hand, I decided to try to capture the joy of a sinking sun. That singular experience changed my life forever.

It began with me sitting at the end of an old wooden dock, weathered gray and barnacled with great green knots. Every once in a while, a fish would splash out of the shimmering waves. The sky was a kaleidoscope of blue and the sun a giant yellow ball.

Slowly the yellows deepened to orange and the sky to a dripping canvas of not only blues but purples and reds and a zillion shades of pink too. Not only did the colors spin differently, but the very texture and design of the sun and water also shifted as the light lowered. Every time I blinked, God repainted a masterpiece.

All the world went perfectly still except for the piercing call of a seagull now and then. The scene was so unbelievably spectacular, it was as if God was putting on a show just for me, just to show me I mattered and He loved me at a time when it was very difficult to love myself.

Like Lehi when he tasted the sweet fruit of the tree of life, I wanted to be able to share this stellar experience with someone

I loved. In the distance, I saw my eldest son walking toward me. He didn't say much. Words seemed so unnecessary as we sat on that dock and watched our loving Heavenly Father put on a light show that no words and not even a hundred photos can adequately describe.

As the clouds wove around and the light lowered, the colors of the sky deepened until we were encased in a magnificent blanket of tangerine pink. Even the water changed colors. And then right before us, at the end of the dock, a shadow moved just beneath the surface. We both watched in wonder as a giant manatee broke the surface.

The Master of the skies. The Master of the water. The Master with whom I ached to converse spoke to me in a way that testified to my soul, not only of His unmatched power and creativity but also of His love for *all* of His children. Including me.

It took about ninety minutes for that scene to go from golden yellow to tar black. But even when the night was thick and the stars were hidden behind a bank of clouds, there could be no doubt about who was in charge.

Oh, how many times have we been too busy to watch a sunset? Or to stop and marvel at the miracle of a moth's wings? We complain that the beach is all sandy. That the desert is so hot. We drive through a majestic mountain range and don't bother to look up. We complain and murmur and groan and simply fail to find that God is waiting every direction we turn with banners and balloons and signs that we are here to enjoy the journey, that we are not abandoned and alone, and, while the road is wrought with danger, it is also lined with opportunity for the greatest adventure ever!

Explorers of Mortality
President Thomas S. Monson, a man who exemplifies joy, calls us all travelers of mortality (see "The Bridge Builder," Conference Report, Oct. 2003).

When I travel, I want to experience everything I can about the people around me—the sights, the history, the smells, the sounds, the textures . . . everything. One of the first things new missionaries at the MTC are told to teach is this: we are on this earth to have all kinds of experiences.

Don't get me wrong. Life is hard. It's challenging. It's disappointing at times. Heartbreaking at others. The world around us is dark and dangerous. As I said earlier, bad things happen to very good people. Good things happen to very bad people. Life doesn't seem fair because it's not fair.

But God is fair. And just. And merciful.

Jesus, the God of this earth, is all of those things plus our Savior and Redeemer. I promise you Jesus is a God of love. He has gone to a great deal of trouble to make this journey through life joyful for us. The Psalmist wrote, "Thou wilt shew me the path of life: in thy presence is fulness of joy; at thy right hand there are pleasures for evermore" (Psalm 16:11).

Dear fellow explorer, here are a few ways for you to find joy in your journey:

1. Be aware of all the good things that already exist in your life.
2. Be excited for the blessings you now seek.
3. Be grateful for life's certainties: for example, the sun will rise and set.
4. Be aware of how many people you love; never take them for granted.
5. Count your friends, old and new.
6. Think about the sound advice people have given you over the years.
7. Reminisce about the wonderful journeys you've experienced.
8. List all the teachers who have successfully taught you.
9. Love the loved ones in your life.
10. Be aware of the good work you do and recognize that it is a blessing to others.
11. Anticipate the items on your bucket list that await you.

12. Count your blessings and realize it's like counting stars.
13. Be keenly aware of your health and how your body can mend itself.
14. Recall challenges that you have overcome.
15. Focus on your faith and not your doubts.
16. Be grateful that you have questions and believe in a God with answers.
17. Cherish the scars you have. They are testaments of your ability to heal.
18. Ask God to remind you of answered prayers, and write them in a journal.
19. Smile at the surprises life has in store for you.
20. Laugh with a child who can remind you what it really means to laugh.
21. Be grateful for energy-packed mornings and exhausted evenings.
22. Savor the taste of fresh-squeezed orange juice.
23. Count the shades of green on a summer day.
24. Close your eyes when you are outside, and really listen to the world.
25. Jot down a list of all the books you've ever read.
26. Be grateful there are libraries of new books you have yet to read.
27. Allow your imagination to run wild.
28. Spend a day exploring textures.
29. Think of the people who have said to you, "I love you."
30. Be alert to your own breath.
31. Phone a friend whose voice you haven't heard in more than a year.
32. Write a letter to release someone you have not previously forgiven.
33. Marvel at a sunrise or a sunset . . . take your time.
34. Soothe a crying baby to sleep.
35. Hold an elderly hand.
36. Beg God to pardon your sins.

37. Create something wonderful.
38. Take advantage of the sacred solitude of a temple.
39. Smile when you're all alone.
40. Bite into ice-cold watermelon.
41. Lie beneath a blanket of stars and let God whisper in your ear.
42. Dance with everyone watching.
43. Forgive yourself.
44. Pray without words.
45. Listen to music that stirs your soul.
46. Lose yourself in the scriptures.
47. Gather your family just so you can embrace them.
48. Nurture your own health and happiness.
49. Let go of the parts of your past that hurt when you hold them.
50. Move forward with faith.

God *wants* you to live a joyful life, even when the world around you is troubled. We know He would not require that if it were not possible. The world's definition of happiness comes when we win a million dollars. It's something that happens to us—an external force. The Lord's definition could be summed up differently. If we work hard, stay honest, use our creativity to earn and save a million dollars, that would be joy. It would not be something that happened *to* us—but that happened *through* us.

If you truly want to live a joyful life even though the world is troubled and unhappy, I promise you it's possible. Bad things have happened in my life, yet I'm more joyful than I've ever imagined possible because I know Jesus does not scowl down on us, whip and chain in hand. Instead, He smiles. He weeps. He runs to us when we call for Him.

The gospel plan is designed so we might have joy. Let's journey together to find ways through the hardships—not just so we can be joyful when we reach the other side but so we can be joyful now, too.

It's possible to be joyful now because the Lord has promised it's possible. "Come follow me," Jesus said. Jesus was joyful. No mortal man ever carried a heavier burden than Christ, yet He found ways to be joyful. He loved. He laughed. He praised. He partied. He feasted. He sought solitude. He sought friendship and love. In essence, Jesus was the ultimate mortal traveler.

Because He has lived a mortal life, Jesus understands how brutal life can be. That's exactly why He assures us that because He has overcome the hardest parts, even death, we can overcome too. We don't have to live in the muck and mire. We can live without shackles or shame. We can be free to live truly joyful lives.

What does all of this have to do with you and your everyday struggles to make the most of your life? Everything. The first principle of joy is to know it is yours for the taking. God wants you to be joyful. "In the world ye shall have tribulation: but be of good cheer; I have overcome the world" (John 16:33).

Be of good cheer.

I have overcome the world.

He's led the way. Now it's up to you to take a step in joy's direction.

Chapter Two
YOUR MIND IS A DOOR

"For God hath not given us the spirit of fear; but of
power, and of love, and of a sound mind."
—2 Timothy 1:7

BET YOU'VE NEVER WOKEN UP in the morning and said aloud,
"Today I am going to suffer. That's the goal: to suffer and be
miserable."

That doesn't happen to most of us. We want to lead
fulfilling and joyful lives. We wake to the world hoping that
the day before us unfolds with joy and miracles—that the odds
are in our favor. We determine the quality of our lives by the
control of our minds.

Think of your mind as the front door to your home. You're
selective about who enters your home. You wouldn't allow
dangerous, poisonous people to come in. You'd shut the door and
lock it against danger. That's what you have to do with your mind.

We Choose What to Believe
Let's go to Liberty Jail, where Joseph Smith was incarcerated.
Liberty, Missouri, was a bustling trading post and the seat of

justice for Clay County during that time. It teemed with people who loathed the Mormons. The governor had issued the extermination order against Joseph Smith and his followers. Apostle David W. Patten had been killed. Winter was upon Missouri with all of its bleakness. And Joseph and his five companions were separated from their families and the Saints, whom they loved, at a time when their leadership was most needed.

The impenetrable jail had been constructed five years earlier, with four-foot-thick walls around the perimeter and the dungeon ceiling barely six feet high. That means that for the four and a half months of a bitter, windy, and snowy winter while he was imprisoned with his companions, Joseph was never able to stand up completely straight while plunged down in a hole he called "hell, surrounded by demons." Only when shown a speck of mercy was he able to come above ground where he could move his lanky limbs freely. His lungs filled with wood smoke when the prisoners were permitted a fire to warm themselves against what records show was one of the coldest winters in the state's history. Joseph was subjected to the crude talk and behavior of his jailers and was constantly exposed to filth in his miserable surroundings.

How, then, did that cramped, freezing, unsanitary jail become a place of spiritual significance? It's something Elder B. H. Roberts referred to as a "prison-temple" (see *Comprehensive History of the Church*, 1:521). How could Joseph meditate in that place and under those conditions? How could he commune with God when the circumstances around him were so wretched? Yet sections 121, 122, and 123 of the Doctrine and Covenants were received while he was incarcerated in Liberty. Even in the grimmest conditions, the man continued to teach and to testify.

Joseph was proven, and he proved to himself, to the Lord, and to the Saints he dearly loved that he was a man of conviction and a human being reliant on God's mercy and strength, even in times of living hell.

It's said of the Prophet Joseph Smith that "only with his body captive could he truly liberate his mind" (Thomas D. and Patricia C. Cottle, "Liberty Jail and the Legacy of Joseph" [*Insight*, 1998], 135–138).

The Apostle Paul talked about renewing the spirit of our minds (see Ephesians 4:22–23). He also promised that we can take every thought captive to obey Christ (see 2 Corinthians 10:4–5).

That's exactly how Joseph remained free even while imprisoned in Liberty Jail.

That's precisely how you and I can remain free when our circumstances would pen us in, smother us with smut, and lead us to believe there is no escape.

Our Thoughts Are Gifts

President David O. McKay referred to thoughts as the "seeds of acts" (Conference Report, Oct. 1951). We don't do something until we've thought about it. That's why a *huge* part of our agency is our ability to think for ourselves. We choose what to think about and what to believe.

Faith isn't merely something we think; it's how we live. What we think and choose to believe creates our faith. It's not something random or arbitrary.

The ability we have to think and reason is a gift from God. The quality of our lives depends on the quality and amount of joy we allow to enter through our minds. The first truth of this book centered on the fact that God has made joy abundantly available to us and that He wants us to live joyful lives. The second truth is that joy enters our lives through our minds. It might dwell in our hearts, but it enters through our thoughts.

Let's consider how this process works: All things are created more than once. Imagine that you are giving your best friend a special party. That party doesn't just happen when guests show up. You create the idea, set the date, and plan the details, such as the venue, guest list, food, and entertainment. You envision the party before it ever happens.

It's the same for a heart surgeon preparing for a triple-bypass operation. She sees herself performing the surgery *before* the patient appears on her operating table. Stephen R. Covey made this concept his second habit: Begin with the end in mind (see *The Seven Habits of Highly Effective People* [Free Press, 1989]).

The reason we humans can do this is because within our skulls is housed a part of our brains called the prefrontal cortex. This allows us to simulate experiences before we have them. It's where precreation occurs. No other creature possesses a frontal cortex.

Pilots have flight simulators that allow them to be trained in all types of circumstances *before* wheels go up. Golfers take a few imaginary swings, seeing the trajectory of the ball, before the club ever makes contact with the ball. When I visited Niagara Falls, I entered a simulator that allowed me to plunge over the falls without ever getting wet. It was a scientific experiment that tricked my brain and body into believing I was falling, spinning, splashing, plunging, and being buried in millions of gallons of cascading water. People actually suffer heart attacks in that simulator because when they go down, their blood pressure goes up. The pseudo creation of that experience is that real.

Why do you think a perfect Designer would give us humans the ability to precreate something? Because He wants us to succeed. Our end result might be a creation that has been created again and again and again and again, each time with us editing, tweaking, and altering. That's okay. That's what the power of the Atonement does—it allows for change.

You Can't Keep Your Thoughts to Yourself

When I was in elementary school, there was a big sign outside the lunchroom door that featured a photo of a variety of vegetables: cabbage, carrots, cucumbers, colorful peppers, and so on. *You Are What You Eat*, the sign read. We used to laugh at that sign and call each other vegetable names.

Now I know what that sign was telling me. If I eat lean, healthy produce, my body is going to reflect health.

The same principle applies to our minds. What we think eventually manifests outwardly in our lives. British author and philosopher James Allen wrote, "Men imagine that thought can be kept secret, but it cannot; it rapidly crystallizes into habit and habit solidifies into circumstance" (James Allen, *As a Man Thinketh* [2012], 56).

If we think happy, kind, healthy thoughts, our lives reflect happiness, kindness, and health. It manifests in the way we live and behave. The same goes for negative thoughts. Medical research has proven that our thoughts are ingrained into our cells and into our very DNA. Repetitious negative thought patterns eventually manifest in physical illness. Because these thoughts are in our DNA, any disease or illness that manifests in us can be passed on to future generations (see Proverbs 23:7).

Isn't it incredible that Heavenly Father has blessed us with the ability to change our thoughts, change our lives, and change our children's lives for emotional, spiritual, mental, and physical health?

You Create the Quality of Your Life

How much time and effort do you actually put into thinking about your own level of joy? Most people fail to contemplate joy in a structured way. Those who do don't let the world's judgment or criticism get them down. Circumstances don't dictate whether their day is good or bad. They dance whether it rains or the sun shines. That's because they have made up their minds to be joyful.

You'll see runners along the road during the most miserable weather. Rain, snow, sleet, or shine, they're there because they made up their minds to run, come what may.

Being joyful isn't something that simply happens. It is a habit we create. We *purposefully* open a door in our minds to allow brighter light and richer experiences to come on in! Joy isn't something that can be purchased or caught; it's a gift we receive as we prepare ourselves to receive it by opening our hearts, our minds, and our lives.

Think of the most joyous person you know. Has that person had an easy life? Most likely not. So what has he or she done to ensure a joy-filled life? Benjamin Franklin supposedly reminded us that the U.S. Constitution doesn't guarantee happiness, only the pursuit of it. You have to catch up with happiness yourself.

That does NOT mean you run after it and hope to tackle it. More often than not, joy thrives best in the everyday, simple things. I've had the honor and opportunity to write about Jesus Christ's life. I've been able to walk the roads He most likely walked. But I didn't have to travel to the Holy Land to understand where Jesus acquired His joy.

Plan A

Jesus worked from a plan. Heavenly Father's gospel is a plan. That means joyful people plan. Of course, mortal plans don't always unfold the way we hope and anticipate, but a joyful life doesn't just happen. It is created. So sit down with yourself and invite the Holy Spirit to guide you as you plan how you want the rest of your life to be from this moment forward. What do you hope to accomplish? How do you want to live? What steps are you going to have to take? Where will the resources come from?

Joyful people are joyful because they are free. They aren't encumbered with debt. So be smart. Plan. If you're already in debt, plan a way out and follow through.

Goals are accomplished in increments and with consistency. If you're not quite sure how to make a plan, start with a prayer. Ideas will come to you, methods will be unfolded, and if you'll seek guidance from God and from people who know how to plan and follow through with a plan, you'll get the life you want.

A Joyful Jesus

Jesus was mindful of joy. Like us, He had one shot at mortality. His was a perfect experience but not because things went His way. He was mocked for standing true to His beliefs. Some of His closest confidants and friends betrayed Him. His short life ended in a torturous crucifixion. Many people looking from the outside in would say He had a sad, even tragic life.

Not so. He was perfect, but because He chose to experience mortality, He subjected Himself to imperfect people and challenging circumstances, to say the least. Our Lord suffered so He could gain complete empathy for our sufferings. Because we all suffer, we should be empathetic with each other. We're all on this journey together. We should be helping each other, not hindering anyone's progress—even our own.

Jesus lived a joyful life because He was mindful of Lehi's teaching: "Men are that they might have joy" (2 Nephi 2:25). Jesus understood that joy is so much more than momentary pleasure, elation, or stewardship of material blessings. Joy lasts. Joy is soul deep. It's a rounded state of well-being, balance, and peace.

Mindfulness, on the other hand, is a practice, a conscientious decision to be present in the moment. If He was with a leper, Jesus wasn't thinking about lunch. We know He wasn't concerned about running out of wine at the wedding in Cana. He was with the guests, enjoying the festivities. It's easy to feel Mary's anxiety, but Jesus understood the power within Him. He didn't fret.

Years ago a teacher instilled in me a how-to-be-joyful lesson that has been passed down through generations: understand the problem, but focus on the solution. We have only so many resources, and if we focus those resources on the problem, we don't have any resources to put toward the solution.

Jesus did this throughout His ministry. He was aware that Lazarus was dead, but He refused to panic. He didn't rush back; "When he had heard therefore that he was sick, he abode two days still in the same place where He was" (John 11:6). He focused on His tasks at hand, foreseeing what was to happen before it happened.

You could safely say Jesus was not a fan of death. He was certainly moved with compassion and anger at death for the sorrow and hardship it caused. But He was in complete control, and Jesus foresaw Lazarus rise *before* he rose. One of the most powerful lessons in all of scriptures is contained in what Jesus did *before* He restored life to His dead friend: "And Jesus lifted up his eyes, and said, Father, I thank thee that thou hast heard me. And I knew that thou hearest me always" (John 11:41–42).

Restoring Lazarus to life was real in the Savior's mind before it was a reality.

That's how to live in joy—anticipate it. Create it. We do that through faith in God's power and in our own abilities.

Jesus also pursued joy by seeking time alone with His Father. In the first chapter of Mark, it's recorded that Jesus spent forty days in the wilderness preparing for His ministry before it officially began. How would our lives change if we spent forty continuous days seeking an audience with Heavenly Father? Or even four days? Or four hours?

What we can learn from Jesus over and over is that He set His mind in place *before* He set His feet and hands and mouth in motion.

We know that as Christ went along doing good, there were times He had to get away from the crush of the crowds—not only those who sought to harm Him but those He loved who also took a toll on Him. "In the morning, rising up a great while before day, he went out, and departed into a solitary place, and there prayed" (Mark 1:35).

It's healthy to spend time alone with the same Father whom Jesus sought—our shared Father. It's also healthy for us to set our minds first, and we do that by opening them to God's will for us.

Jesus went to the mountaintops, into the desert, and out onto the water so He could be alone. There were times He spent all night in prayer (see Luke 6:12).

If you study closely, you'll see that when Jesus was physically and emotionally spent, He sought solitude with God. He did it after He fed the five thousand. When He heard of John the Baptist's death. Even in the Garden of Gethsemane, Jesus withdrew from His chosen disciples to be alone with His Father, to gather the strength to do what He knew He had to do.

How does this translate into a lesson for us? We all need to seek and spend time with God—*alone* time. Not many of us have the option of a forty-day trek into the wilderness, but we can rise up early in the mornings, spend a night on our knees, or seek Him in the temple or the pages of the scriptures.

George Washington Carver is attributed with saying, "I love to think of nature as unlimited broadcasting stations, through which God speaks to us every day, every hour, and every moment of our lives, if we will only tune in" (*George Washington Carver: In His Own Words*, ed. Gary Kramer [1991], 143).

Want to feel simple, powerful joy? Look at a tree. Now look at a different type of tree. And yet another tree. Watch birds in flight. Get down on the floor and frolic with a puppy. Lay back and observe clouds as they move across the sky. Study the stars at night. All of existence is joyful for those with open eyes to see. The other day I rode my bike up a canyon and stopped by a pond to watch a beaver family busy building a dam. What surprised me most wasn't their industriousness. It was the fact that they stopped to play. To splash and chase each other. Nature, as harsh as it can be, is simply joyful.

Trees, plants, birds, animals, and all of nature is joyful because all of it fills the measure of its creation without worrying about money, prestige, or health or anything but existing in the moment. Only humans get distracted by such things.

Those who have lived and experienced life realize money can purchase a house, but it cannot build a home. It can buy a book, but it cannot give you knowledge. It can buy a bed, but it cannot bring sleep. It can pay for medicine and doctors, but it cannot buy health any more than purchasing a clock will buy you time. Money will never bring lasting joy. You will find joy only in the things money cannot buy.

One philosopher observed how marvelously joyful flowers are. Have you ever seen a flower that wasn't happy? That's because it's true—God is in the details, and spending time in nature is spending time in the midst of God's efforts and creativity on our behalf. It's there we can feel His perfect, magnificent love for us.

This world was created for our advancement, pleasure, and utter joy. Can you imagine how Heavenly Father feels when we return to Him and report that we missed the beauty and the majesty and the gift that life really was?

We don't have to wait until we feel our joy wane before we seek time alone with God. We can do it when we are overflowing with joy. "Heavenly Father, I've come to be with you because I'm so blessed, so happy, so full, and I just wanted to express my gratitude."

If we live to be seventy-five years old, we get roughly twenty-five thousand days and nights. Surely we can dedicate some of those to the God who gave us life in the first place. Can you think of a better way to renew your mind and spirit?

Jesus gained much joy from spending time with people. Relationships brought meaning to His life. We know He shared a lasting bond of friendship with Lazarus. We know He loved John, the cousin who baptized Him. Jesus loved Mary and Martha. He bonded with Peter's mother-in-law by serving her and allowing her to serve Him in return.

He cherished His disciples, especially the Twelve He chose to follow Him. He was loving to their families. He showed compassion to the masses and to individuals.

When we spend time with people who make us think, our minds expand and our lives broaden. When we are around people who live joyful lives, that joy tends to infiltrate our lives.

We tend to become like the people with whom we spend the majority of our time. Try a little experiment. Mindfully seek out people who challenge you to be better. To live higher. Notice that those people seldom talk about other people. They talk about concepts and methods and wonders. They don't sit around. They move. They are authentic human beings full of life, compassion, and joy.

We Can Change Our Thinking

A study of the life of Jesus teaches us we can change our lives when we change our thoughts. Isn't that what faith is—a change of thought in preparation for a change of heart? We see it every time a nonbeliever comes to believe.

Peter, Andrew, James, and John were fishermen who anticipated that their lives would revolve around the shores of Galilee. In part, the four cousins were right—but not as men who caught fish. When their thoughts aligned with the Master's, they became fishermen who brought the souls of men to salvation. They thought it was impossible to walk on water, to heal the deaf and blind, to rise from the dead *until* their minds were changed and enlightened by the power and reality of Jesus.

Writer and humorist Erma Bombeck discovered that she was dying. Instead of trying to be funny, she wrote of her regrets. If you read carefully, you'll see what she saw—relationships with others and with ourselves are what matter most and where joy is found in abundance. Oh, how she wished her thinking had changed earlier in her life!

> If I had my life to live over, I would have talked less and listened more.
>
> I would have invited friends over to dinner even if the carpet was stained and the sofa faded.
>
> I would have eaten the popcorn in the "good" living room and worried much less about the dirt when someone wanted to light a fire in the fireplace.
>
> I would have taken the time to listen to my grandfather ramble about his youth.
>
> I would never have insisted the car windows be rolled up on a summer day because my hair had just been teased and sprayed.

I would have burned the pink candle sculpted like a rose before it melted in storage.

I would have sat on the lawn with my children and not worried about grass stains.

I would have cried and laughed less while watching television—and more while watching life.

I would have shared more of the responsibility carried by my husband.

I would have gone to bed when I was sick instead of pretending the earth would go into a holding pattern if I weren't there for the day.

I would never have bought anything just because it was practical, wouldn't show soil or was guaranteed to last a lifetime.

Instead of wishing away nine months of pregnancy, I'd have cherished every moment and realized that the wonderment growing inside me was the only chance in life to assist God in a miracle.

When my kids kissed me impetuously, I would never have said, "Later, now go get washed up for dinner."

There would have been more 'I love yous' . . . More "I'm sorrys" . . .

But mostly, given another shot at life, I would seize every minute . . . look at it and really see it . . . live it . . . and never give it back. ("If I Had to Live My Life Over," Dec. 2, 1979)

Jesus did not live with regrets because He paused to be with people. He knew what mattered. He knew what rendered joy. He never had to change His mind because He never took His eye off the prize. He did that by keeping His thoughts in line—

by consciously thinking, "What is the end result I want? What is the wisest use of my time?"

Jesus found joy in right-intentioned service. His entire life was a reflection of service. Yes, He performed mighty miracles, but we don't have to heal the blind to make a difference in someone's life. He was conscious of His motives. You can see that in the way He stopped to help hurting people and in the way He listened to them. Jesus was a gifted listener. He invested the most precious of all commodities—His time—in the lives of others.

He went in search of people who most needed service. While others avoided the Samaritans, Jesus crossed the borders into the land where citizens were despised. To them He brought the good news of the gospel. He went to the lepers. He sought out the lame. He listened to the lonely. And He did not esteem anyone above anyone else. All people were worthy of His time and service. The Romans. The Jews. The foreigners. The lost. The rich. The poor.

His thoughts aligned with His acts. He knew that joy didn't come from the absence of pain, hardship, and suffering. It came through the acceptance and endurance of victory over those burdens. That's when true change came.

The Prophet Joseph Smith taught that when our minds and hearts are changed and filled with the love of God, we want to expand our service beyond our own circle. We become anxious to bless the whole human race (see *History of the Church*, 4:227).

Here's a secret about service. We go into it thinking we are going to bring joy to someone else, but service is the gift that gives back. Try spending time in a children's hospital. You can't come out of there without tears on your cheeks and joy in your heart. True joy comes when we attempt to bring joy to others. To lose our lives, taught the Savior, is to gain life.

The Indian writer and painter Rabindranath Tagore observed: "I slept and dreamt that life was joy. I awoke and saw that life was service. I acted, and behold, service was joy."

One of my most joyful memories is the time I spent sitting next to a painter in India. Leprosy had stolen the man's fingers and turned them to stubs that were unable to hold a paintbrush, so he painted with what was left of his toes.

His beloved pet cow was there too, swishing her tail at flies and sometimes into the paint. The man did not stop smiling the entire time I was with him. He saw beauty in blue, red, yellow, purple, and orange and in a paint-speckled cow. He taught me to see beauty in those things too.

Our circumstances might not seem joyful, but if our thoughts are, then what do our circumstances matter? Our primary reason for unhappiness is not our circumstances but how we think about them. Imagine if Jesus had not maintained a positive attitude. What if He had looked around at His circumstances and given up?

Jesus found joy through *prayer*. Do you realize you can pray for an abundance of joy in your life? You can pray for a change of mind. Elder Bruce R. McConkie taught that "spiritual gifts are endless in number and infinite in variety" (*A New Witness for the Articles of Faith* [1985], 371). Joy is a gift for which you can pray. Today. Right now. You can ask, "Father, please let joy enter my mind, my heart, and my life. Let me do the things that will make a joyful life possible."

One of the greatest joys comes when our prayer lives reflect our outer lives. Corrie ten Boom was a devoted Dutch Christian who became the first female watchmaker in her native Amsterdam. Her life was one of service. She never married and stayed devoted to helping her family. She also ran a church for mentally disabled people, raised foster children in her home, and was extremely active in other charitable causes.

Along with her father and other family members, Corrie helped many Jews during the Nazi horrors of World War II. She was imprisoned for her actions and suffered unthinkable acts of suffering. She could have become the most bitter, unhappy woman in the world. But Corrie realized the exact same thing Jesus and Paul realized when they were behind bars—enemies could imprison her body but not her thoughts. Those she could send heavenward: "I kept on praying to dispel my fear until suddenly and I do not know how the idea came to me I began to pray for others. I prayed for everyone who came into my thoughts—people with whom I had traveled, those who had been in prison with me, my school friends of years ago. I do not know how long I continued prayer, but this I do know—my fear was gone. Interceding for others had released me" (Corrie ten Boom, *Amazing Love: True Stories of the Power of Forgiveness* [2006], 61).

Watch Your Thoughts

Our thoughts determine our direction. Are we headed toward joy, or are we turned in a different direction? The Apostle Paul is a stellar example of a person whose changed thoughts changed his life. When Paul wrote to the Romans, he was an expert at thought control. He could have turned bitter and angry at the treatment he was receiving, not just from his enemies but from negligent Church members too. How easy would that have been? They promised him support and didn't come through. They left him to suffer in the worst imaginable ways. He could have conceded to fear. Instead Paul transformed his life (not his circumstances) through the power of Christ's Atonement. The Atonement gives us power to change, and that's what Paul talked about—to be changed inwardly and not by our outer circumstances. "And be not conformed to this world: but be ye transformed by the renewing of your mind, that ye may prove what is that good, and acceptable, and perfect, will of God" (Romans 12:2).

There's an old adage: you are as happy as you make up your mind to be. *You* can design a joyful life—actually, you're the *only* one who can design a joyful life for yourself. You choose to be grateful, to be ambitious, to be dedicated, to be obedient to God's commandments. Choose your thoughts, and your actions follow.

That's easy to believe when things are going your way. But let death or sickness or an economic tumble take place and see just how difficult it is to stay positive in the midst of negative circumstances.

Then there are people who are depressed without knowing why. One woman I spoke with talked of having a faithful, loving husband, healthy children, financial security, and the gospel of Jesus Christ. "It didn't make sense, but I was so unhappy. In the end, I had to lose myself to find myself, but God never left my side during the entire journey."

The reason God suffered is so He can succor us if we will allow Him to.

A passage in Alma 50 teaches us all that if we are faithful obedient and continue to try to do what's right, to align our thinking with Christ, we can be joyful no matter our circumstances. If we are not, we can change through the power of repentance.

Oh, what a harrowing time is recorded in the middle of Alma! Moroni was making preparations for war against the Lamanites. His armies were digging pits and building picket timbers around the tops of the city walls. Watchtowers and strongholds were being erected because enemies were at the borders, bloodthirsty and infused with hate. Moroni's leadership kept his people industrious, building new cities, fortifying the old, and strengthening the armies.But the Lamanites were not their only enemies; within their own ranks, there was mutiny, quarreling, contention, murder, plundering, idolatry, whoredoms, and abominations.

Yet those who were faithful to the commandments were prosperous and "delivered at all times." In fact, the record states something astonishing: "There never was a happier time among the people of Nephi, since the days of Nephi, than in the days of Moroni" (Alma 50:22–23).

Never a happier people, even though they were surrounded by enemies who sought to kill them. Never a happier people, even though they battled constant internal strife.

Think of the lessons we can learn from this example. As long as we live the gospel to the best of our ability, as long as we repent when we need to, we can have protection and blessings. We can correct and straighten our crooked thinking and our crooked lives.

Yes, you say, but what of the times when bad things happen to us and those we love, even when we are striving so hard to live obediently? Then we go back to what the woman above said: "God never left my side."

Guard the Door

It's up to us to guard the door of our minds so unwanted thoughts don't enter. Inevitably, they will. That's why the Lord has also provided a back door. In they come; out they go! We have the ability to sweep them out. How? With positive, powerful thoughts. In essence, we think about our bad thoughts with good thoughts.

You can create a thought. Entertain it. Change it. You can make that thought into a reality. Your ability to think is a precious gift.

We choose how to live by the thoughts we choose.

We change the course of our lives by the *new* thoughts we choose to follow.

What we must never do is drive out an old, nasty, negative thought and then leave a void in its place. The devil will be right there to fill any void with his ugly, depressing, dangerous thoughts. So nudge out the old and replace it with something new and better.

Positive, hopeful thoughts are great! We need to nourish them and nurture them. To ponder them. But what about the negative thoughts that bully us? Here's a thought—a friend of mine kills her negative thoughts and buries them. Literally. Let's say she's going to a job interview and the negative thought enters her head: "You're not going to get hired."

First, she recognizes that a negative thought has invaded her mind.

Second, she captures it—sometimes with imaginary pinchers, sometimes with a SWAT team, sometimes by imagining herself marching up to that thought and nabbing it.

Third, she tells the thought why it has to go.

Fourth, she executes the thought.

Fifth, she buries the thought with an imaginary funeral.

Sixth, she does not resurrect the negative, destructive thought. It's gone for good.

It might be a silly exercise to some people, but for her, it works.

Life is difficult. Some people seem to face hardships with courage and come out stronger for the struggle. They are able to climb impossible mountains in their lives. Others seem to be unable to recover from difficulties and end up bitter, blaming others or God for their misfortune or just sinking into depression. The ones who survive and even thrive in spite of challenges are often those who have faith in God, who trust Him to help them through tough times. Here are some thoughts you can use to affirm a mighty change of mind:

Jesus is joyful. Therefore, I can be joyful too.

I choose which thoughts to dwell on and which thoughts to bury.

When bad things happen in my life, I can reach deep into my humanity and let them bring me closer to Christ by seeking new understanding.

I will look to Christ in every thought (see D&C 6:36).

Out of my mouth flows life and death. I choose life.

Even when I sin, I am still loved beyond measure.

There is always a way back. That way is Jesus Christ.

No matter how lonely I may feel, I am never alone.

When I am not worthy, I can become worthy through repentance.

Things will improve.

I am capable of greatness.

Procrastinating only extends my pain.

It will get better.

Guard the door with all diligence. Be aware of the thoughts you've already allowed to enter your mind. Sweep out the ones you don't want taking up residence. Fill your mind with thoughts about Christ and His way of thinking. Think like Jesus thinks. "A noble and Godlike character is not a thing of favor or chance, but is the natural result of continued effort in right thinking, the effect of long-cherished associations with Godlike thoughts" (Allen, *As a Man Thinketh*, 11).

Chapter Three
WHO'S IN CONTROL?

"Yet he who reigns within himself, and rules passions,
desires, and fears, is more than a king."
—John Milton (*Paradise Regained*, Book 2
[London: n.p.,1817], 42)

SNAKE CHARMING HAS BEEN OUTLAWED in India. Still, you can see these street performers in most of the cities where tourists have money. One man in Rajasthan, India, appears to have complete control over a massive king cobra. When coiled in its basket, the serpent fills the entire thing, top to bottom. When the lid comes off, the snake immediately uncoils, extends its hood, and rises to a startling, if not terrifying, height. The charmer sways as he plays his pungi, and the snake undulates with him, seemingly entranced.

A gathering of onlookers is mesmerized and rewards the man's control of the serpent with a toss of coins onto a collection plate.

Only there is nothing really brave about the occupation of a snake charmer. And there is certainly nothing magic. For starters, this man's cobra, like almost all street-performing snakes, has been defanged and its venom drained. Also, cobras don't have ears, so when the serpent appears to be swaying to the rhythm of the music, it's really moving in response to the motion of the charmer's leg and pungi. To the cobra, both appear to be rival snakes. If the cobra fails to rise and sway, the man has a sharp stick he uses to agitate the snake.

For days, maybe weeks, the snake has been fed a milk diet; since the cobra can't digest milk, it is slowly being poisoned so it will be more manageable. When it rises from its lidded basket, it does so because it's been trapped in darkness. Its natural instinct to the sudden bright light is to rise and spread its hood, alert to danger.

The entire show is an illusion—a lie to make tourists believe the charmer is a courageous man capable of controlling a venomous viper with only music and dance.

Now you know the truth. Yes, the charmer controls the snake, but at what price?

Once, you and I witnessed another street performer try to control us. In our premortal lives, we attended a grand council where Satan did his best to convince us that if we would allow him to control us, he would march us through mortality and return us all to the presence of God. Glory be Satan's.

But Father had another plan—a perfect plan that allows us agency to control our thoughts and acts. We choose whether we will follow the laws, keep the commandments, and honor the covenants of God's plan.

God's plan of choice leads to joy. Satan's plan of control leads to misery.

Who's Steering This Thing Anyway?
Do you want to know how to lose your joy? Try to control everything and everyone around you. My uncle called it herding cats, and it's insanity that leads to an out-of-control life. Nothing causes more stress than trying to control what is not within our realm of control.

At a recent conference, I asked the audience, "Do you know who parted the Red Sea?"

"Moses!" a thousand voices replied.

"Nope. God parted the Red Sea. Moses was a prophet, an instrument, the man with the staff, but it was God who performed the miracle."

Of course, they already knew this, but sometimes we forget who is really in control.

Our lives lose the chaos and fear when we remember who is really steering this thing we call life. Our modern-day prophets have promised us that God is at the helm. A *helm* is the apparatus used to steer a ship. There's a well-known country music song called "Jesus, Take the Wheel." It's about a young woman who has tried to steer her own life and realized how impossible that is and now begs Jesus to take control and save her as her car hits black ice.

God is in control. Never doubt it. Trust Him in all things, including how to live a joyful life. When we are confronted with opposition, when we freeze with fear, He will be there to make a way when there appears to be no way. In his April 1994 general conference address, President Gordon B. Hinckley taught that though "our individual efforts may be humble and appear somewhat insignificant, [our] accumulated good works . . . will bring to pass great and wondrous accomplishments." We can be happy and blessed with the Lord "leading us through pastures green and peaceful, if we will walk after His pattern and in His light" ("The Lord Is at the Helm").

Control versus Responsibility

Knowing what you can and should control and what you can't and shouldn't control is a key to living joyfully. Trusting God in all things is the way we can live joyfully in a world filled with suffering, fear, and uncertainty.

The choice at this crossroads is to know that God is in charge of the masterpiece but the brushstrokes are ours. In other words, we live with hope, knowing that in the end all things that are unfair will be made right. The big picture will make beautiful, blissful sense. For now, though, we are mortal, we live in a fallen world, and the responsibility to be joyful in spite of all of that is ours.

The world blames circumstances. We know better. We are responsible for our thoughts, our actions, and our levels of joy.

"Arrrg!" the Laman in me says. "Arrrg!" the Lemuel in me says. "How can I be happy when I'm living in the wilderness? When I'm being deprived of life's comforts? Trials are everywhere I turn. Life's not fair!"

Nope. It's not.

We are responsible for the state of our lives—not our circumstances, not our relatives, not our friends, and not our employer. If we're joyful, that's because we choose to be joyful. If we're sad, that's because we choose to be sad.

Wait a sec. Back up. Stop! It's time we camp together and talk about depression among members of the Church who choose to be happy but who still suffer depression, anxiety, and other forms of mental illness.

It's okay. You can breathe. It's okay. You can weep. It's okay. You can heal and be happy. My qualification for addressing this matter is personal experience. I've suffered debilitating depression.

Experts told me disappointment triggered my depression.

Maybe. Who hasn't been disappointed? Here's how sneaky Satan is: he waits and watches for disappointment to come. Then he does everything in his power to keep us in that state of sadness. If we stay down, disappointment leads to discouragement. Discouragement leads to despair. Despair leads to depression. After that it's a whirling cycle that's hard to stop spinning.

King David, a fellow who knew a whole lot about depression, wrote something that gives us hope: "Weeping may endure for a night, but joy cometh in the morning" (Psalm 30:5). Things may make us feel sad temporarily, but we must not stay sad. We can't allow our circumstances to control our emotions.

Satan knows when to strike. He knows when to plant doubts and fear. He came to Jesus when Jesus was weak from a forty-day fast. "*If* thou be the Son of God . . ." IF? He tried to make Christ doubt His divine identity.

Oh, the devil is a sinister demon. He is a discourager, and he and his demonic armies work to pull us down emotionally, spiritually, financially, and in every way. Jesus, on the other hand, is our encourager. He lifts us. He brings peace. He speaks the language of hope.

Emotions can be our enemies. Even joy. Why? Because we are easily led by how we feel. But feelings change in a blink and for a plethora of reasons. Let's take a look at three examples. First, from the book of 1 Kings: Elijah, the great and mighty man of faith, has managed to call down fire from heaven. He's won a great victory at Mt. Carmel over the prophets of Baal, the Canaanite false god. For the moment, he's elated. Elijah's emotions are soaring. The Israelite leaders who witnessed this demonstration seem to have turned to God, and God has ended the drought. No wonder this prophet is on an all-time high.

After a few verses, Elijah has outraced Ahab to Jezreel, where he undoubtedly anticipates Ahab and Jezebel's repentance or surrender or defeat.

Blink, and the prophet who was the epitome of spiritual courage has now run away and collapsed into a sobbing heap of depression. How could a man so committed to God, so utterly happy, fall so hard and so fast? It's worth reading and pondering the entire story, but for now, let's focus on the first verses of chapter 19:

> And Ahab told Jezebel all that Elijah had done, and withal how he had slain all the prophets with the sword.
>
> Then Jezebel sent a messenger unto Elijah, saying, So let the gods do to me, and more also,

if I make not thy life as the life of one of them
by to morrow about this time.

And when he saw that, he arose, and went
for his life, and came to Beer-sheba, which be-
longeth to Judah, and left his servant there.

But he himself went a day's journey into
the wilderness, and came and sat down under a
juniper tree: and he requested for himself that
he might die; and said, It is enough; now, O
LORD, take away my life; for I am not better
than my fathers.

And as he lay and slept under a juniper
tree, behold, then an angel touched him, and
said unto him, Arise and eat.

And he looked, and, behold, there was a
cake baken on the coals, and a cruse of water
at his head. And he did eat and drink, and laid
him down again.

And the angel of the LORD came again the
second time, and touched him, and said, Arise
and eat; because the journey is too great for
thee. (vs.1–7)

Elijah, the prophet with God's power at his beckon, is now
a suicidal mess. But don't give up on him yet. Let's pause here
because we have all felt at times that the journey before us is too
great.

There is a moving hymn in our LDS hymnal penned by
President Joseph Fielding Smith and entitled, "Does the Journey
Seem Long?" The story behind that hymn is very much related
to the story of Elijah. And it's our second example.

Joseph Fielding Smith was a member of the Quorum of the
Twelve Apostles at the time. Because Church business called
him away much of the time, his second wife, Ethel Reynolds

Smith, was responsible for her husband's two children from his first marriage and what would amount to seven more of their own. This was almost a hundred years ago when there were no automatic washers and dryers, grocery stores on the corner, freezers, and fast-food solutions to "What's for dinner, Mom?"

There were no disposable diapers. No flushable wipes.

There was no prescription available to help balance the brain's chemicals.

In the spring of 1924, when Ethel was seven months pregnant and suffering greatly, her husband was on a train headed to preside at a stake conference. He pulled out a pen and paper and wrote to his wife, "I am thinking of you, and wish I could be with you constantly for the next few weeks, to help take care of you." He then set his pen down and rested his eyes. He blinked them open, picked up the pen again, and wrote:

> Does the journey seem long,
> The path rugged and steep?
> Are there briars and thorns on the way?
> Do sharp stones cut your feet
> As you struggle to rise
> To the heights thru the heat of the day?
> Is your heart faint and sad,
> Your soul weary within,
> As you toil 'neath your burden of care?
> Does the load heavy seem
> You are forced now to lift?
> Is there no one your burden to share?
> Let your heart be not faint
> Now the journey's begun;
> There is One who still beckons to you.
> So look upward in joy
> And take hold of his hand;

He will lead you to heights that are new.
(*Hymns*, no. 127)

How can a man know a woman's heart? Perhaps in that moment of concern and love for Ethel, Joseph was inspired with a glimpse. After all, they were both engaged in the crucial work of building the kingdom—hers quite different from his but both crucial.

In time, Joseph would go on to become President of the Church, while Ethel would go on to suffer "a terrible illness which she could not understand" nor could she cure. Bouts of mania and severe depression led to her hospitalization. She tragically died in 1937, leaving behind children who still needed her (see *Teachings of Presidents of the Church: Joseph Fielding Smith* [2013], 1–34).

This story is not as uncommon or as tragic as it seems. But the story doesn't end when tragedy strikes, because Jesus Christ won the victory over death and depression. Life isn't as long as it seems, and separation for those who are sealed for time and all eternity and who honor their covenants is not final.

God's plan is perfect. Therefore, it allows for mortal trials like depression and mental instability.

It's easy for someone who has never suffered depression to prescribe a cure. It's quite another thing for the Lord to prescribe a cure. For me, that cure was to move my body, exercise my mind, and be still and come to know God. The journey was long and seemed impossible at times, but that's when God's miracles become manifest—when life seems impossible.

We don't have all the answers.

It's not for us to judge another.

It is for us to love and seek to understand.

Let's return to the story of Elijah. The angel didn't mock Elijah, scold Elijah, or condemn Elijah. He ministered to him—physically and emotionally.

Empowered, the prophet,

> . . . arose, and did eat and drink, and went
> in the strength of that meat forty days and forty
> nights unto Horeb the mount of God.
>
> And he came thither unto a cave, and lodged
> there; and, behold, the word of the Lord came
> to him, and he said unto him, What doest thou
> here, Elijah?
>
> And he said, I have been very jealous for
> the Lord God of hosts: for the children of Is-
> rael have forsaken thy covenant, thrown down
> thine altars, and slain thy prophets with the
> sword; and I, even I only, am left; and they seek
> my life, to take it away.
>
> And he said, Go forth, and stand upon the
> mount before the Lord. And, behold, the Lord
> passed by, and a great and strong wind rent the
> mountains, and brake in pieces the rocks before
> the Lord; but the Lord was not in the wind: and
> after the wind an earthquake; but the Lord was
> not in the earthquake:
>
> And after the earthquake a fire; but the Lord
> was not in the fire; and after the fire a still small
> voice. (1 Kings 19:8–12)

It was in that still, small voice that I found my way out of the darkness. When faced with the pain and horrors of divorce, I kept a reel playing in my head that reminded me, "Be still and know that I am God. Be still and know that I am God."

This became my mantra. It became the scripture that proved to be a true and faithful friend. It became my lifeline at a time when I felt there was no one to save me and nothing to grasp.

The Holy Spirit yearns to communicate with us, to bring us comfort. That's the very purpose of the Spirit. But when we have the television blaring or we're blasting music or talking nonstop, it's impossible for the Spirit's still, small whisper to be heard.

As you heal, as you seek to be made whole, you will crave silence. It won't be a terrifying place where you have to hear your own insecurities and come face-to-face with them. How can you heal what's wrong if you can't hear the Spirit teach you what it is that needs to be mended? Trust the silence. Trust the Lord's love for you. Listen for His voice.

Don't overlook the fact that to feel better, Elijah slept. Twice he slept, twice he ate, and twice he drank. If you're physically exhausted, hungry, and dehydrated, you're susceptible to trouble.

Depression creeps in when we neglect ourselves.

The other day while I was walking with a friend, she asked me if I understood the greatest commandment.

"To love the Lord. Our neighbors. And ourselves."

She stopped. "To love the Lord first . . . and then?"

"Our neighbor," I said.

She frowned and pointed out that the next part of the commandment was to love our neighbor *as* we love ourselves. "That means *because* we love ourselves, we can and should love our neighbor," she said.

I went home and found this wisdom in Mark 12:28–31:

> And one of the scribes came, and having heard them reasoning together, and perceiving that he had answered them well, asked him, Which is the first commandment of all?
>
> And Jesus answered him, The first of all the commandments is, Hear, O Israel; The Lord our God is one Lord:
>
> And thou shalt love the Lord thy God with all thy heart, and with all thy soul, and with all

thy mind, and with all thy strength: this is the
first commandment.

And the second is like, namely this, Thou
shalt love thy neighbour as thyself. There is
none other commandment greater than these.

My friend was right. We are commanded to love our
neighbors *as* we love ourselves.

Who doesn't struggle to love themselves? We all do,
but knowing how important that is on the Richter scale of
commandments, we can all try a little harder to be a little kinder
to ourselves, to care for our needs and wants, and to forgive our
flaws and mistakes more readily and completely.

And now for our third example, which illustrates that no matter
how much we love God, ourselves, and our neighbors, sometimes
things just don't go the way we plan. When that happens, we find
ourselves susceptible to disappointment, frustration, and sadness.

Epaphroditus was a faithful Christian who loved Jesus
and the gospel. We don't know specific details of his life, but
we know he was a devoted man, a willing man, and a joyful
man who took up the dangerous task to tend and bolster the
imprisoned Apostle Paul. It fell to Epaphroditus to deliver
money and whatever else the Saints had gathered.

Paul's love for this man is evident. The circumstances and
details of what happened are unclear, but we know that after
he was in Paul's presence, Epaphroditus fell ill to the point of
death and distress, and it seems Paul ended up taking care of
him and ultimately had to send him back.

This is the gospel in full action. The Philippians were concerned
with Epaphroditus, Epaphroditus with the Philippians, and Paul
with both. But nobody was concerned with himself. The goal was
service, not selfishness (see Philippians 2:25–30).

Oh, what joy this Church would know if we could love
and care for each other without judgment and in humility!

Paul admonished his fellow Christians to "support the weak" (1 Thessalonians 5:14). Real friends, Paul taught, are those "born for adversity," and they truly stay at the side of a depressed person (Proverbs 17:17). When the Apostle Paul felt laid low and afraid, he was comforted by the presence of Titus (see 2 Corinthians 7:5–6).

The bottom line is this: none of us is completely free from the onslaught of mental illness. Each of us has a sacred duty to love and support those who suffer. What lesson about control can we learn from the well-intended servant, Epaphroditus? Life throws us the most ironic and unexpected—not to mention unwanted—curves. How we deal with them is a test of our faith and an opportunity to enable us. It helps us stay in control of what falls within our stewardship and step away from what doesn't.

In such a topsy-turvy situation, Epaphroditus entertained some pretty negative thoughts. He erased in his mind all the previous good he had accomplished because he was now physically sick and could no longer tend to Paul. Today we'd call that depression.

The Lord understands the fact that depression, regardless of its cause, is not our choice. It's a trial to overcome. And it can be overcome with the right care and understanding. If you suffer depression, give yourself a break and get all the help you can—but if you are a person who simply chooses gloom over glory, well . . . stop it and make better choices.

Self-Control

Maybe you feel like you have no control over your own life. Perhaps it seems like whatever is meant to happen is going to happen, so why should you bother trying so hard?

If God is in charge of the ship, the ocean, the weather, the skies, the planet, the universe, and beyond, what does that leave to the captain? Plenty. The care of the ship. The protection of the crew. The cargo. The passengers. Supplies. A watchful eye toward the weather. Charting of the course. And so on.

Contrary to what Satan would tell you, your choices *do* matter. You are free to decide for yourself how you handle what life hands you. You choose.

First and foremost, the captain is in charge of himself. Self-control means governing ourselves. It's mastering our weaknesses and joining with God to turn those weaknesses into strengths.

Unfortunately, self-control is a difficult skill to master. The University of Pennsylvania surveyed two million people and asked them to rank their strengths in twenty-four different skills. Self-control ended up in the very bottom slot. Only the smallest fraction of those people considered their lives joyful.

What does self-control have to do with joy? When it's gone, so is your productivity. Without productivity, we feel lazy and worthless. Joyful people don't fight Jesus for the steering wheel. They beg Him to take control—to guide, inspire, and protect. In the Alcoholics Anonymous program, we say, "Let go and let God."

That's when we surrender and find freedom. Freedom is joy.

My grandma used to teach her grandchildren that what someone else thinks of us is not our business. She often told us, "You can't control another person's feelings or thoughts. You can only control your own."

When I was a small girl, I came into Grandma's house one day crying because my cousins were being mean to me. Actually, I was doing a little more than simply shedding tears. I was wailing, shaking, and getting ready for a fight.

"They make me so mad!" I bellowed.

"They can't make you mad unless you let them," Grandma announced. She had me sit down and made me drink steamed milk with black pepper and butter in it. (It's a Danish thing.) When I had regained a little of my self-control, Grandma said, "The person who gets you to act like you just did is the person who controls you. Is that how you want to live the rest of your life?"

Then she pulled out the big black Bible she kept in the bathroom and read a proverb from the Old Testament: "He that is slow to anger is better than the mighty; and he that ruleth his spirit than he that taketh a city" (Proverbs 16:32).

We give up our control in many ways, and when we do, we forfeit our joy. We fought a war in heaven for the chance to make our own choices. Why on earth would we fight God now?

People in Dire Circumstances Can Still Be Joyful

Following a tsunami in Southeast Asia, I walked along the beach, navigating my way through miles of wreckage. I looked up toward the city and realized how many homes, businesses, and lives had been lost. The sadness I felt at the devastation forced me to find a piece of driftwood and ease myself down on it to let the surge of emotion pass through me.

While I sat there, head tucked, heart breaking with the now-gentle waves, I heard the most unexpected sound. Someone was laughing. Another someone joined in. I bolted upright and whipped around to see a family scalloping the same shoreline, headed right for me.

I watched as they frolicked in the lapping, foamy water. I listened as the children squealed and the father chuckled. One man. Three small children, including a baby in his arms.

They were on some sort of scavenger hunt. I wasn't sure what they were looking for, but the largest boy carried a basket, and every few moments someone would put something inside that basket. At first I wondered if they were collecting seashells. But they weren't. They were scavenging for anything that they might use to rebuild their lives and a home that had been bludgeoned to splinters and washed out to sea.

As we talked, the father explained that his wife and two more of his children had been swallowed in the cruelty of that ravenous storm.

I joined them and walked along, picking up boards, corrugated tin, a single flip-flop that fit the young girl, an empty soda can. Soon we were joined by many, many others who were searching through the debris washing in with the tide.

Our language skills didn't exactly mesh, but I asked, "How can you still be so happy?"

They didn't seem to understand what *happy* meant, so I smiled. They returned my smile. I laughed. They laughed louder. Pretty soon we were a laughing multitude of people in the most horrendous circumstances.

Eventually the father pointed out to sea, drawing my attention to a sheet of now-placid blue water, a perfect reflection of a cloudless sky. Shaking his head, he said, "Control? No."

I took away from that experience many lessons, but the main thing I learned was that we are very small next to an ocean. We have absolutely no control over the ebb and flow of the waves. Yet we're important to the One who created and controls all of it.

There was a moment standing there, sinking in warm sand, feeling the sun on my face, and listening to people who had lost everything still laugh with each other, when I surrendered to my Higher Power. At that moment, I let go of the insane idea that I was in control of my life.

God is in control of my life. I realize now that He has given me a spirit of self-control, but that doesn't mean I get to control anything other than myself.

What Joyful People *Do* Control

When you come to know that God is at the wheel, steering your life in the direction it needs to go—the way that leads back to Him—it's easier to trust life. That's not saying you don't have a responsibility for your own salvation. You most certainly do! You are saved by grace *after* everything you can do, so let's concentrate on what joyful people do to control what they should and trust God to control the rest.

Joyful people mutter. Not mumble. Not murmur. They mutter positive words all day long, whispered prayers and words of affirmation to themselves. Apart from Christ, I can do nothing, "but with God all things are possible" (Matthew 19:26).

Joyful people are observant. The simple act of noticing the good things in your life improves your outlook and helps you see God's hand in all things—good or bad.

Joyful people open their hearts to gratitude. They are aware of their vast resources—material, human, and spiritual—and make the most of them through gratitude and use.

Joyful people do good. They look for opportunities to improve their own lives and the lives of others.

Joyful people reboot. When they feel themselves falling, they do what Jesus did to reboot—they spend time alone with God.

Joyful people hang on. They don't let go, especially when the ride gets rough. Joseph Smith is attributed with saying, "Never be discouraged. If I were sunk in the lowest pits of Nova Scotia, with the Rocky Mountains piled on me, I would hang on, exercise faith, and keep up good courage, and I would come out on top" ("Memoirs of George A. Smith," typescript copy, BYU Special Collections, Harold B. Lee Library, Provo Utah, 36).

Joyful people are kind to themselves. They say things like, "I've got a great laugh." "I like my eyes." "I am capable of learning new things." "I am a loyal friend."

Joyful people live in order. The Lord's house is a house of order. A house of chaos breeds contention. Joyful people aren't afraid of confrontation, but they strive to live in peace.

Joyful people progress. "To be or not to be?" is *not* the question. What is the question? The question is not one of being but of becoming. "'To become more or not to become more.' This is the question faced by each intelligence in our universe" (Truman G. Madsen, *Eternal Man* [1966], 32).

Joyful people don't take offense. They don't get worked up over small things . . . and they work out big things, unafraid to confront when necessary. They are courageous without being contentious.

Joyful people make their own choices (with God's counsel). If you don't decide for yourself, someone else will decide for you. Don't let that happen. Value your agency.

Joyful people remember who they are. Joyful people remember what they stand for, and they act accordingly in all places and at all times. Miserable people are chameleons. They change depending on who they are around. If they're with commandment keepers, they act one way; if they change audiences, they act differently. This kind of life is not only miserable, but it's also exhausting.

Joyful people pray but realize the answer is not always going to be yes. They trust God, even when He says "Wait" or "Nope, not this time." They move forward in faith. They trust not only that God knows best but also that His love for them is why they don't always get everything for which they ask. It's not a matter of bitterness; it's a matter of becoming better.

Joyful people work productively. They don't see labor as a burden but as a blessing to make them stronger, to build confidence, and to produce good, useful, and creative results.

Joyful people ask for help. Joyful people know they can't go it alone, so they ask for help—not only through prayer but also from other people. They are direct and don't beat around the bush, try to manipulate, or drop hints and hope someone understands and comes to their rescue. If they need help, they yell, "Help!"

Joyful people release the need to be right. Prideful people cannot be joyful people any more than faithful people can be fearful people. The two ends don't meet in the middle. A joyful life requires a total release of pride. Peeling pride off a spirit is like peeling superglue off of skin—it hurts *a lot*.

In *Mere Christianity*, C. S. Lewis wrote that the proud cannot know God because a "proud man is always looking down on things and people: and, of course, as long as you are looking down you cannot see something that is above you" (New York: MacMillan, 1952, 108–109).

Joyful people learn. They learn from successes and mistakes what worked and what didn't work. They don't learn from their own experiences alone; they're smart enough to learn from others' experiences too. That's how better decisions are made.

Joyful people don't stand at the door. When one door closes, they realize it's not always a bad thing. They realize if it was meant to stay open, it would have stayed open. So they move on.

Joyful people live in the moment. They learn from the past and plan for the future but live in the present.

Joyful people adopt an eternal perspective. This is something we need to address many times. God promises to make all of us well if we only believe. But He doesn't promise that will happen right now, in this life on earth. Some prayers get answered in heaven. We will be able to trust God when we focus on the fact that this life (along with its struggles and pain) is temporary but heaven is eternal. And we know that for those who love God, "all things work together for good" for those who are "called according to his purpose" (Romans 8:28). That might not bring much comfort now, but it will over time if we remind ourselves that God's timing is not ours.

Loss is right up there at the top of reasons why people are unhappy. But people who believe in a hereafter deal with death in hope rather than despair. Charles Dickens penned it with an eternal perspective: "The pain of parting is nothing to the joy of meeting again" (*Life and Adventures of Nicolas Nickleby* [London: Chapman and Hall, 1839], 22).

Joyful people compete with no one other than themselves. If you're always in a hurry, always trying to get ahead of the other guy, or being motivated only by someone else's performance, then that person is in control of you (see drwaynedyer.com).

Joyful people forgive. This is a big one. Joyful people master forgiveness because they practice it all the time. They are quick, and they are thorough. If someone injures you and you choose not to forgive, you allow that person to hold your future joy hostage. Until you let go of your pain and anger, you can't enjoy the present. Therefore, whenever you refuse to forgive, you hold yourself back from living the joyful life God wants you to live.

It's true what writers have written a hundred different ways: the best form of revenge is your own joy and ability to move on with life.

Joyful people don't try to change other people. Leo Tolstoy summed it up when he wrote, "Everyone thinks of changing humanity, but nobody thinks of changing himself."

That's what we really should focus on controlling—changing ourselves.

It's Not Really about Control

Joyful people control what is within their stewardship and responsibility to control. They may influence some outside of that circle, and they may show care for things they can't control, but their resources are spent controlling what they can and leaving God at the helm, trusting Him to be captain. When they do that, they can stop worrying about everything. Stop fretting. Stop spending their time and care on things that are not theirs to control. That's when they can focus on being joyful. That's when they can finally feel truly free.

Chapter Four

Unhappy Things Will Happen

"When it is dark enough, you can see the stars."
—Ralph Waldo Emerson

THE FIRST MOMENTS OF YOUR life as a new parent brim with joy—and terror. In that moment when a new baby is first placed in your arms, your capacity for love expands like the earth being torn asunder. Though your heart might grow and grow, with that growth comes a crack, and in that crack comes an icy black fear that the child you love so very, very much might one day, somehow, be lost to you.

I have this child. I'm overjoyed.

I could lose this child. I'm terrified.

It's the dichotomy of parenthood. I *did* lose my firstborn child, so I know something of that never-goes-away pain. I learned that without pain there would be no suffering, and without suffering we would never learn from our mistakes. I also learned that through Christ, joy can exist in the most tragic times. Joy can exist at *all* times if we don't let go of our Savior's hand when we need Him most.

Have you ever stopped to realize that events don't cause our sadness—emotion does. If you get reprimanded by your boss and you come home in a bad mood, you might say, "It's because my boss is a jerk." But what's really going on? It's not the event that caused you to feel the way you do; it's the emotion attached to the event. At first you might have been embarrassed, then later, angry. Now your mood is foul, and you think it's your boss's fault. But it's the emotions that are playing you, not the event.

Certain events can and do trigger emotions, but emotions are what you're feeling and what you should identify. Most of us don't stop to consider what we are feeling and why; we just blame events.

So if you tap into joy in the face of a loss, you can shift your emotions. When my mother died, I remember taking a night to climb out of the sadness long enough to talk about the fun and funny memories. That exercise let me attach joy to an excruciatingly painful time. You can do the same with gratitude. Stop and think of what you have to be grateful for in a sad situation. It will move things around and allow you to identify what you're feeling, separate from what happened.

We're not talking about laughter or elation. We are talking about peace and hope and a sure promise that life does not end at the grave, and all that unfairness will be made fair somewhere along the plan's outlay.

The truth of this life is that if we live long enough, we all fall down. We all break and wear out. We all suffer sorrow and loss. We all need the Lord's balm.

When you travel through parts of Africa and the Middle East, you'll encounter shops that sell a soothing salve called the Balm of Gilead. *Balm of Gilead* is referred to three times in the Old Testament. As Joseph's brothers were contemplating how to kill him, a caravan of Ishmaelites rolled by on their way from Gilead to Egypt. In their cargo were "spicery and balm and myrrh" (Genesis 37:25).

After hearing God's warning to Judah of what Babylon would do to the chosen land and people, Jeremiah laments, "Is there no balm in Gilead?" (Jeremiah 8:22). His question is a poetic plea for healing that led Edgar Allen Poe to reference it in his poem "The Raven."

Later in the book of Jeremiah, there is an impending punishment due Egypt. "Go up in to Gilead, and take balm, O virgin, the daughter of Egypt: in vain shalt thou use many medicines; for thou shalt not be cured" (Jeremiah 46:11).

I testify to you that no matter what your pain is, regardless of who caused your wound, there is a healing balm in the Atonement of Jesus Christ and in His perfect love. The Great Physician of our spirits and bodies, Jesus told His earthy disciples, "They that are whole have no need of the physician, but they that are sick" (Mark 2:17).

One of the reasons Jesus came to earth was to heal. If we will allow Him to do that, we too can be made whole.

None of Us Remains Unscathed

Imagine if your bishop stood before your ward and asked, "Will everyone who has never known pain or sorrow please stand up?"

How many people do you suppose would rise to their feet?

Sundays are the days we dress our best. We put on clean, pressed clothes. Women wear makeup. Men shave. We sport our nice jewelry. We smell of cologne and perfume. We do our hair. Why all the fuss? We do it to show respect for ourselves and our God but also to put on our best appearance.

But God looks upon the heart, not the clothes and the shoes and the show.

He sees the sorrow we hide with smiles.

He sees that Brother Over There has just been diagnosed with Alzheimer's disease. He knows that the Hansens have just had another argument and are both contemplating divorce. He knows one of the young priests struggles with sexual orientation. He knows the widow on the back row has contemplated suicide. He knows that Brother Perez just lost his job and that Sister Perez will be laid off next week. He knows Sister Sharon will never bear children. God knows who is in debt over their heads. Who is being abused and who is abusing. He knows who carries the weight of sin that has not been repented of. Who hides secrets. Who bears burdens so crushing they can't stand up straight. In his "Choruses from The Rock," the poet T. S. Eliot wrote it as poignantly as any pen could:

> You neglect and belittle the desert,
> The desert is not remote and southern tropics.
> The desert is not only around the corner
> The desert is squeezed into the pew next to you.
> The desert is in the heart of your brother.

Just because we're smiling doesn't necessarily mean we're happy. But God wants us to be happy in spite of bad things that come. His grace is sufficient to see us through the hard times. Even when bad things happen, joy can exist in abundance. Our darkness can be diminished, even vanquished, through the transforming power of Christ.

Transformation in our lives begins when we engage with Jesus Christ. It happened with the woman at the well. She and Jesus engaged in conversation. It happened with the woman who brought oil to anoint the Master. It happened with the lame man lying next to the pool at Bethesda.

I love the story of the man at the pool because it has so many aspects and can be interpreted many ways. However, the intent of the Savior cannot be misunderstood—He was there to heal.

"Would you be made well?"

The man's response had to be a yes or a no. Either he wanted to get healed or he didn't. Until I actually visited that site and saw the pools and learned the story, I didn't realize that if the man had said yes, he would have had to give up his life of begging and the income that came with it. If he had said no, he would have remained with everything familiar.

It's the question Jesus asks of all of us. Do we really want to be healed of whatever is keeping us from living the joyful life we are meant to live?

Are we willing to give up the misery that garners us attention?

Are we willing to put in the hard work and sacrifice that is always required?

Do we truly want to pay the price that a joyful life demands? Because we have to live on purpose. We have to be willing to seek joy.

I can't speak for anyone else, but I know I don't want to stay depressed for a second longer than I have to. When I'm sick, I am anxious to be well again. I don't want to stay down. I want to be moving, doing, and living!

Hope to Be Healed

For joy to exist, there has to be hope. I can imagine how dismal the crippled man's hope was after thirty-eight years. Every year tradition said the pool was stirred by an angel and that the first to enter would receive healing magic. And every year, someone else beat the man to the water. *Every* time for thirty-eight years running.

You'd think after thirty-eight years the man could have inched his way to the water. Instead, he stayed in the same spot and mourned his ill fate.

Then Jesus came along and didn't even offer to put Him into the pool. Because Jesus *is* the living, healing water. He is the miracle. He is the magic. The man was healed and Jesus told him to take up his bed and walk. In essence, he says, "Clean up the mess you've made in all this time and move forward."

That's the message I get out of that story: God works. We clean up and move on. That was the message in my life when I lost hope. I don't share my personal life with you for any reason except to give God glory for what He has done to save my family and me, just as surely as He did the man at the pool in Bethesda. Years ago my eternal marriage came to an unthinkable and abrupt end. I was left with a quiver full of wounded, hurting children who were asking, "Is there any hope for us?"

This was when I had to separate my emotions from the event. Though our situation looked utterly bleak, it wasn't—because God can restore hope in the most hopeless situation. I can promise you that Christ is the way through crisis. No matter what you're going through, you don't have to go through it alone.

Spending time working in prisons and with the homeless youth of the world has given me insight into what true suffering is. I feel blessed, but I understand that sometimes the greatest lessons about how to live joyfully come from the most tragic stories.

Sunken Hope

A week before Christmas 1927, the S-4 was conducting routine drills just off Long Point, Provincetown, when it surfaced and was inadvertently rammed by a U.S. Coast Guard destroyer. The ship sliced a two-and-a-half-foot hole in the starboard side of the submarine, and the U-boat sank rapidly into 110 feet of icy water.

You can imagine the frantic moments that followed as the crew attempted to stop the flooding but were ultimately forced to retreat behind watertight doors. Most of the sailors ran toward the rear of the submarine and soon drowned. Six men ran forward to the torpedo room, where they faced a less compassionate end.

On the surface, a massive effort was launched to try to save the sailors. It became an international news headline as navy and coast guard experts tried several times to raise the stricken submarine. Divers descended to the wreck and used a hammer to tap messages on the hull in Morse code; in response, they received replies from the trapped crewmen.

Near the end of the ordeal, a deep-sea diver who was doing everything in his power to find a way for the crew's release thought he heard a tapping on the steel wall of the sunken sub.

He placed his helmet against the side of the vessel and realized he was hearing Morse code. He attached himself to the side and listened in anguish as the question from within was tapped out: "Is . . . there . . . any . . . hope?"

The diver was tragically forced to reply, "There is none."

"We . . . understand," came the reply.

More than anything, I wish I could tell you the rescuers found a way to save those trapped men, but all forty men aboard ultimately died.

Is there any hope?

That is a question we will all utter at some point in our lives.

When our prayers tap out that question, the Savior will never reply, "Nope. Out of hope for you and yours."

With Jesus, there is *always* hope. "Blessed is the man that trusteth in the Lord, and whose hope the Lord is" (Jeremiah 17:7).

The scriptures are filled with stories of people who had hope in Christ and found relief from pain, were granted miracles for the asking, and received forgiveness through the mercy of Christ.

I couldn't find any tales of people who approached Jesus and were turned away. Or denied. Or times when miracles failed. But I talk to lots of people in the work I do who tell me of times when their prayers went unanswered, when the miracles they sought never came. They describe the chilling distance they feel between them and God.

The scripture teaches, "To some is given the working of miracles" (D&C 46:21; see also 1 Corinthians 12:10; Moroni 10:12).

For me, the miracles come not in being healed, not in being saved, but in remaining faithful, even—and especially—when the miracles we seek don't come the way we beg for them to come. That's when our faith is truly tested and rewarded.

I know I would never wish divorce on my worst enemies. But in the darkness and hopelessness of my experience, I found hope and light. I felt the Savior's love in a way that words can't express. So I'm thrilled to testify that He is there for *all* of us *always* if we will invite Him and trust Him—even when the outcome we want doesn't unfold the way we want it to.

Prayer Is Our Hope

The Psalmist penned it perfectly: "Attend unto my cry; for I am brought very low" (Psalm 142:6). When unhappy things happen, prayer is the first and best resource we have. But it doesn't come without a price, and our answer doesn't always come in the way we think it should.

One woman was a longtime member of the Church. She married in the temple, picturing a joyful life. Thirty years later she was in prison, serving a life sentence without the possibility of parole.

"God never heard my prayers," she told me. "For thirty years I begged God to save me, to change my husband, to do something. He never did."

The woman was bitter and in obvious pain as she told her story. I wrapped my arms around her and held her, promising her that God did hear and answer prayers.

"Not mine," she said, drawing away.

I was with a group of volunteers, among them LDS priesthood holders called to serve in the prison. Priesthood blessings of comfort and guidance were available to this group of women, to any who so desired. While the others scrambled to take advantage of the opportunity, my friend stayed on her chair, head bowed, eyes wet with tears, fists clenched tight. Nothing I could do or say could persuade her to believe that no matter what, she could still commune with her all-loving, all-knowing Heavenly Father.

I went home and studied prayer. I wanted to understand how a woman could pray as fervently as she had and still feel that God had gone silent when she most needed to hear His voice.

I learned the following:

We should strive to be worthy to pray, but unworthiness will never be a barrier to sincere and honest prayer. Because I'm a sinner, I know God hears the prayers of sinners with a quick ear.

Prayer is the ultimate source of guidance, comfort, relief, and protection.

The Creator of the Cosmos commands, "Thou shalt pray vocally as well as in thy heart; yea, before the world as well as in secret, in public as well as in private" (D&C 19:28).

We can pour our hearts out to God anywhere, anytime.

If you can, prepare for prayer by seeking out the right place of solitude, pondering what you want to talk over with God, and making your mind and heart open to any inspiration that might come. *Expect* it to come.

We don't have to worry about a prescribed manner of prayer as much as we do about a humble, sincere heart. Let the words pour out of your mouth, but make sure they come from your heart.

Prayer becomes more effective when we ask not for what we want but for what His will is for us. "Father, what should I do?"

Our part of prayer is to "study it out in [our] mind" (D&C 9:8). When we do this, we usually don't get a single big-bam answer. Answers come as thoughts, guidance from the Holy Ghost, and sometimes through the help of other people. I know someone who often receives inspiration through dreams. The beautiful thing about this concept is that God knows how to best communicate with His children on an individual basis because each of His children is of individual worth and deserves individual attention.

God expects us to do our part. Most answers come as gentle nudges or new ideas, requiring us to consider, contemplate, experiment, sometimes struggle, and then act in full faith, expecting God's guidance all along the way.

Most prayers are rewarded as we offer our agency, humility, and faith. When the answer is complete, we can look back and see that it was given to us line upon line, a little here and a little there as we exercised our faith and moved forward in love. This testifies to us that personal revelation—answers to prayers—comes in direct proportion with our preparation to receive it.

When our prayers seem to go unanswered, that's when we need to step up our game and pray more fervently, more gratefully, and more openly. We can't give up on prayer. Not momentarily and not ever. Pray even when it seems that heaven isn't listening.

When we have no desire to pray, we need to be humble enough to simply bend our knees and stay down until we feel prompted what to say and what to do. If all you do is bend and bow and wait, that's enough. Let God do the rest. When it's time, you'll know when to rise and move on.

Answers to prayer rarely arrive while we're on our knees. Inspiration and guidance, comfort and peace come later as we move in faith as if the answer is before us. When we're still, we can best hear the Spirit speak to us. God speaks when it's quiet.

Answers don't always come in the way we want them to, and the answer is sometimes *no* when what we ache to hear is a *yes*. That's when we have to pray for God's wisdom and trust that He knows what's best for us now and eternally.

Too many times our prayers are advice to God. We tell Him what we think He needs to do. Effective prayers begin with an admission that we are powerless to solve some of our own problems but we're willing to try anything God directs.

He will let us struggle as we strive to find answers to our prayers, but He will never leave us in those times of struggle.

The more you exercise faith, the stronger your faith becomes and the more effective your prayers are. It's an awesome cycle!

Sometimes prayers are answered with promptings *before* you even ask. Go back to the moments before Jesus raised Lazarus from the dead.

A friend once asked me how it's possible to tell if the answer to prayer is really from God or if it's just a conjecture of our own minds. The Lord answered that twice: "Ask me if it be right, and if it is right . . . your bosom shall burn . . . ; therefore, you shall *feel* that it is right. But if [what you present] be not right you . . . shall have a stupor of thought" (D&C 9:8–9; emphasis added). Also: "I will tell you in your *mind* and in your *heart*, by the Holy Ghost" (D&C 8:2; emphasis added). The answer isn't just a thought but also an accompanying feeling that the thought is right.

Often that feeling is simply peace. Remember Oliver Cowdery's concern and the Lord's answer: "Did I not speak *peace* to your mind concerning the matter?" (D&C 6:23; emphasis added).

Sometimes you won't feel peace, you won't sense a confusing stupor, and you won't feel anything at all. This is what my inmate friend said she experienced. This is what she mistakenly took for an unanswered prayer when it was really a trust from God in her. In the talks that followed our initial conversation, she told me she knew what she should have done—she should have taken her children and left her abusive husband. She could have gone to a shelter, a Church member, a relative. "I should have trusted that God trusted me," she told me. "I should have moved forward in faith. Looking back, I can see that He was telling me, 'I'm here for you,' all along."

Sometimes God will allow us to make a mistake, but He won't let us proceed too far before His Spirit prompts us to turn around. That's the point of Elder Jeffrey R. Holland's talk and video illustration *Wrong Roads* (lds.org [2013]). It's the point of Lehi's "opposition in all things" speech. We have to know one to appreciate the other.

The most insightful prayers begin and end with expressions of gratitude. Disciplining yourself to account for your blessings puts an immediate positive perspective in your mind. A friend who lost her grown daughter said that being able to pray with gratitude was the factor that got her through her mourning period. "We were blessed with her for twenty years. In those twenty years we made such wonderful memories. We learned so much from our daughter. And we can be grateful for the knowledge that covenant families, by the sealing power of the priesthood, will be reunited on the other side of the veil. Without that assurance, I'd go insane."

If life is so hard that it's difficult to see the blessings that surround you, beg God for eyes to see and a heart that can still beat with gratitude even in the midst of loss and pain and sorrow.

Laughter Is Medicine

Laughter is a powerful antidote to combat stress, conflict, and pain. Nothing puts out-of-whack spirits back into alignment like a good laugh. So let's stop here and read some letters children wrote to God. They understand life better than we do. These excertps from an array of letters children wrote to God and from conversations they had with parents about life give us lots of reasons to smile—as well as a few that make us stop and think:

Dear God, instead of letting people die and having to make new ones, why don't you just keep the ones you've got now?

Dear God, in Bible times, did they really talk that fancy?

Dear God, I think about you sometimes, even when I'm not praying.

Dear God, I didn't think purple and orange went together until I saw the sunset tonight. Good job.

Dear God, I bet it is very hard for you to love all of everybody in the whole world. There are only four people in my family, and I can never do it.

Dear God, please put another holiday between Christmas and Easter. There's nothing good in there right now.

Dear God, if you watch in church on Sunday, I'll show you my new shoes.

Dear God, I would like to live nine hundred years like the guy in the Bible.

Dear God, what happens when you die? Do you just melt into the dirt like a popsicle?

Dear God, we read Thomas Edison made light. But in Sunday School they said you did it. So I bet he stole your idea.

Here's a great statement overheard at a restaurant: "Why do they call *them* waiters when *we* are the ones who wait?"

When a big sister asked the Taco Bell manager why chicken cost more than beef, her five-year-old sister piped up, "Because chickens are harder to catch than cows."

When a little boy heard the Bible story of how Lot was warned to take his wife and flee out of the city but his wife looked back and was subsequently turned to salt, the child was concerned and asked, "What happened to the flea?"

My favorite one is probably the kindergarten girl who asked her grandmother how old she was.

"I'm so old I don't remember," the grandmother replied.

"If you don't remember," the girl said, concerned, "you'd better look at the back of your panties. Mine says five to six."

They Will Happen

While a positive outlook and a lot of laughter can carry you through difficult times, they cannot prevent negative things from occurring.

Sad things.

Bad things.

Unfair things.

We don't discoverer what we're made of or who we really are until things don't go our way. Only under fire can gold be refined.

When your world shatters with the loss of a loved one, the dissolution of a relationship, or a massive disappointment, remember that the love of God is joy. Separation from God is sorrow. What does that mean? God will bring you peace. He will bring you healing. He will stay by your side until your tears have dried. To think you can or that you have to suffer alone will bring only more suffering.

We can't go around the things that challenge us; we must go *through* them. That's how we grow, and it's how we grow closer to God. Like the biblical heroes Shadrach, Meshach, and Abed-nego, we get to know God when we spend time in the fiery furnace with Him (see Daniel 3).

Even Jesus wasn't spared the "going though" part: "If it be possible, let this cup pass from me: nevertheless . . ." (Matthew 26:39).

Nevertheless.

How Does Sorrow Seep In?

We all know that life is hard. It was designed to be hard. Our own choices often invite pain and suffering into our lives through sin. We don't know *how* the infirmed man came to lay beside the Bethesda pool. We only know the length of his incapacity—thirty-eight years.

Once Jesus gave him fresh legs and a new life, He gave the man an even greater miracle: a pardon from sin. A spiritual restart. The point that Jesus wants to drive home for this man and for us is that no amount of healing—physical or emotional—is going to make any real difference for us if our spiritual health is not restored. Anything else is just a temporary fix. That is ultimately what Jesus came to do. What each of us has spiritually wrong with us is ultimately and eternally fatal. But Jesus came to restore us to spiritual health. Jesus wants to help make us spiritually strong so we stay true and joyful even when bad things happen.

Wickedness never was happiness (see Alma 41:10). It never will be happiness. It might lead to pleasure, but pleasure is physical and temporary. Happiness is a good thing—but even happiness is not a lasting thing. It's just an emotion that will fade and change and come again.

Joy, on the other hand, is a state we can maintain even in the midst of trials with the help of Christ.

So if there is sin at the root of your suffering, do whatever it takes to let God clean your life and restore you to spiritual health.

God *Will* Give You More Than You Can Handle

Go back two thouand years to a small church in the city of Corinth. The people there loved the Apostle Paul and cherished the letters he sent to them. In one of his first, he wrote about temptation. He understood that as strong as we want to be, we all fall prey to temptation. He wrote, "There hath no temptation taken you but such as is common to man: but God is faithful, who will not suffer you to be tempted above that ye are able; but will with the temptation also make a way to escape, that ye may be able to bear it" (1 Corinthians 10:13).

This verse has been misquoted so many times it's infuriating. For starters, let's clarify that Paul was referring to temptation—not suffering. With temptation, we always have a choice: to sin or to turn around and run away. (Think of Joseph in the Pharaoh's courtyard.) The promise Paul makes is that if we want to run, Heavenly Father will always provide a way for us to escape sin.

Nowhere does that promise apply to suffering. We don't get to choose which trials we face. The wife whose husband is struck and killed by a drunk driver. The baby who dies of cancer. The faithful spouse who endures divorce.

Jesus suffered the ultimate pain so that He can empathize with us, no matter what it is. Even if you think He doesn't understand, He does. Even if you fear He will turn away, disappointed or disgusted, trust His compassion, His empathy, and His mercy.

What about His judgment? It will be loving and fair, and we can't ask for more than that.

When the fear, despair, and pain grow so powerful we think we can't survive, know that others have felt the same way. The Psalmist poses the same question Christ posed while dying on the cross: "Why hast thou forsaken me?" (Psalm 22:1). We all feel forsaken at times. "Lover and friend hast thou put far from me, and mine acquaintance into darkness" (Psalm 88:18).

Think of Joseph Smith in Liberty Jail. He found a way to be free even when he was behind bars. His soul was filled when his belly was empty. I don't see it as a coincidence that it's named *Liberty* because Joseph learned what Jesus wants to teach us all: we will suffer, sometimes more than we can bear alone, but He, the God who loves us best, will suffer with us and see us through. Darkness may surround us, but it is the light of Jesus Christ that is our closest, truest friend, the friend that will not fail us.

I've seen people die from trying to carry their burdens on their own shoulders when Christ stands ready, arms out to help us bear the weight that has been placed on us. Think of my inmate friend.

Not all suffering is a result of sin. A lot of it is simply life. Bad things happen to very good people. Life isn't fair. Nowhere are we promised that it will be fair. We are promised only that it will be joyous to those who strive to keep the commandments, repent when they don't, and keep on trying.

It's okay—it's human—to feel that we are not going to make it, that we might as well give up. When our souls are overwhelmed and death seems welcome, I believe specially assigned angels wait to hear our cry. They stand ready to help if we will cry for help. When we do this, the Savior suffers with us.

Please, in your pain, don't forget that Jesus is called our Savior because He saves. His entire life and death and Resurrection stands as a testament that you are worth saving. Call out. Call loud. And don't stop calling until you know you've been heard.

What Joyful People Do When They Hurt

Joyful people suffer, but don't become bitter. They somehow become better. Why? Because they don't go it alone. They team up with the Coach. And their questions become:

Why not me?

What can I learn from this?

Am I grateful for what I have instead of focusing on what I don't have?

How can I grow closer to Thee?

The prophet Isaiah spoke of God's love for us, especially in times of trials: "My kindness shall not depart from thee, neither shall the covenant of my peace be removed, saith the Lord that hath mercy on thee" (Isaiah 54:10).

Like everything else, choosing to stay joyful in unhappy times is a choice we must make not just once but over and over because life is not going to stop testing us until the Savior says, "Well done."

Chapter Five

ONE BRICK AT A TIME

"Success is to be measured not so much by
the position that one has reached in life
as by the obstacles which he has overcome."
—Booker T. Washington
(*The Booker T. Washington Reader*
[Radford, VA: Wilder Publications, 2008], 23)

IMAGINE THAT YOU ARE STANDING in front of a brick wall. It's high and it's wide. On one side of you is a barren landscape. On the other side is a lush land of joy and peace. As you look at the wall keeping you out of that joyful land, you realize you laid every single one of those bricks.

Please give this exercise some sincere effort. Study your wall. Picture each individual brick. Ask yourself what is keeping you from living the joyful life God intended you to live. Imagine standing back and seeing just how wide and tall your wall is. Now move in closer. Closer. Move so close you can see the color and texture of each individual brick and the mortar that is holding it in place. Now imagine that each brick is labeled.

Forgive me for being personal, but I when I was nearly a half century old, I was able to dismantle the majority of my brick wall. I'd like to tell you about one brick in particular.

I didn't know how to swim. The fact that I couldn't swim made me feel insecure and unhappy and maybe even a little ashamed. I could not make it from one end of a pool to the other. I could dogpaddle from the center to the side, so I could play in the pool with my kids, but I just couldn't make my body glide through the water. I felt like a failure. Every little kid learns how to swim. Every adult I knew could swim. Even when I eavesdropped on the children's swimming lessons and attempted to implement the skills they were learning, it just didn't work for me. I swam like a rock.

There's a reason for my lack of swimming skills. When I was about six or seven years old, I would wander our city streets and make my way to a local public pool. I would climb to the highest diving board and tiptoe my way to the edge of the board. Then I'd plug my nose and jump.

I'd plunge down into the deep water, holding my nose until my body bobbed to the surface. Then I'd dogpaddle to the edge of the pool, pull myself up, run back to the diving board, and go through the entire process again and again.

Only one day while I was down at the bottom of the pool, waiting for the water to bob me back to the surface, a big teenage boy didn't realize where I was, and he dove headfirst off that diving board.

We cracked skulls beneath the water.

An ambulance and a hospital stay were involved. For a very long time after that, I was terrified to get into a swimming pool. The next time I entered the water was in an ocean; a school of jellyfish attacked me, and a lifeguard had to rescue me.

Now reel ahead four decades.

I took my metaphorical wall of bricks—the barriers separating me from my idea of joy—one brick at a time, to God. He didn't laugh at me or mock me. He didn't tell me my method was stupid or silly or that it was too late to change. He was simply there for me. In the previous chapter, we addressed how important it is for us to do our part so the Lord can do His. Well, I went out and bought a pair of plastic fins. I purchased a pair of goggles. I enlisted my swim-savvy friends for help. For the next three years (yes, *three* years), I struggled to make it from one end of the pool to the other.

Oh, I got so I could maneuver up and down the pool like a dolphin but only as long as I was wearing my plastic fins. In fact, my nickname became Fins. I was really proud of my accomplishment, and my friends thought I could swim, but I knew that without those floppy plastic feet, I'd sink.

Then one morning when it was so early that I found myself the only swimmer at the pool, I realized I'd forgotten my fins. I jumped in anyway, thinking I'd revert back to dogpaddling, frog kicking, back floating, or whatever. But something happened three-quarters of the way up the lane. I felt an impression whisper, "Swim." I did what I'd done a million times without success: I thrust out my arms and my legs. I expected to sink. Instead, I swam—arms, legs, gliding through the water. I made it to the end, turned around, and swam to the other end!

Glory hallelujah! If someone had seen me in those moments, they would have thought all that water on my face was from the pool—but those were tears of joy and gratitude cascading down my cheeks.

I was celebrating a true brick-breaking miracle.

I want you to have those spectacular moments too. That means you have to examine each brick and know what's blocking you so you can dismantle your wall brick by brick.

The Center Brick

When groups of men, women, and youth were asked to identify some bricks that keep LDS people from feeling joyful, they repeatedly mentioned one in particular. It is a BIG brick, smack-dab in the center of almost everyone's wall. It is our inability to be perfect, even though we are commanded to be just that: "Be ye therefore perfect, even as your Father which is in heaven is perfect" (Matthew 5:48).

I don't know about you, but I'm not acquainted with any perfect people. I have more flaws than just about anyone I know. I'm so far from perfect that that commandment seems unattainable, yet it isn't—because God would never command us to do something without providing a way for us to accomplish it (see 1 Nephi 3:7).

Elder Bruce R. McConkie told an audience of BYU students that no one becomes perfect in this life—only the Lord Jesus Christ attained that state because He had an advantage that none of us has. He was the literal Son of God in the flesh. Elder McConkie reminded students that becoming perfect is a process, and it starts with keeping one commandment, perfecting it, and then moving on to the next and the next . . . all with the Lord's help (see "Jesus Christ and Him Crucified," *BYU Speeches*, Sept. 5, 1976).

Moroni taught how to do this bit by bit, steady as she goes: "Come unto Christ, and be perfected in him, and deny yourselves of all ungodliness; . . . and love God with all your might, mind and strength, . . . that by his grace ye may be perfect in Christ" (Moroni 10:32).

Oh, how I love the word *grace*! By His grace . . . His enabling power, His mercy, His all is made available to us. Those of us who attempt to do it on our own will inevitably fail and find ourselves miserable.

Also, if we believe that immediate perfection is expected, we'll become disillusioned and discouraged in our inability to measure up. The Lord even counseled Joseph Smith: "Do not run faster or labor more than you have strength and means" (D&C 10:4). Like Joseph, we are not required to do more than we have strength and means to do. Nor do we have to become perfect in all things *right now*. The Lord is a lot more patient with us than we tend to be with ourselves.

If we attempt to go it alone or try to run faster than we should, all kinds of bricks go up, adding their mass to our wall: depression, self-doubt, failure, humiliation, compulsive behavior, addiction, and ruined relationships, to name a few.

Never once does Jesus say, "I am the wall." He says, "I am the way. The door. The gate." He is the opening for us to return home to the Father. His way leads to a joyful life, and you can believe that He will help us tear down our walls brick by brick.

Other Bricks

Another brick many people mentioned was a **lack of total commitment** to a variety of things but mainly to the Lord. Spiritually straddling between the Lord's way and the world's way is deadly. We might be able to pull it off for a season but not forever. It's just too exhausting.

You've heard it. Maybe you've even said it: "I want to be spiritual. I want to live righteously. It's just that I'm human."

Of course you're human.

Lighten up. The Lord's way is hard but not impossible. "Take my yoke upon you, and learn of me; for I am meek and lowly in heart: and ye shall find rest unto your souls" (Matthew 11:29). We take His yoke upon us when we admit we can't do it alone, when we ask for His help and accept it.

You are not alone. The Lord is not as concerned about perfection as He is growth. He knows your heart. He is aware of your unique and individual circumstances. He loves you and is mindful of all aspects of your life, challenges, and limitations. You don't have to worry and build a big fat brick to stand between you and joy just because you haven't reached the spiritual pinnacle where you'd like to be. All you have to do is keep trying to progress. A simple rule that has helped me says, "If it's good for you, do it. If it's not good for you, don't do it."

The Lord sees that you're climbing. He sees that you fall and get back up and try again. He's there to help and to remind you that the plan is not for you to make it without Him.

Comparison is another brick we put up. We see how sharp our neighbor looks, how many smiling vacation pictures he posts on the Internet, and how much joy he seems to experience in comparison to the difficult and sometimes dull life we live.

His life isn't perfect. No one's life is as joyful as it looks on Facebook.

Anxiety is another common brick. People get anxious and worry about the things they can't control. It doesn't matter how much you worry. It doesn't matter how much anxiety you bring to a problem. Neither one of those things is going to make one bit of difference to the outcome. Break down that brick by remembering to let go and let God.

Judgment is yet another common brick. We all have a deep need to be accepted and loved by others. For those of us who have suffered abuse, we tend to worry about what people think and say behind our backs. One negative comment or whispered rumor can crush us. The brick-breaker for this is to forgive quickly and completely and to focus on what *God* thinks of us, not on how people judge us. No one but God can know our hearts. Letting God alone define our worth will bring a whole new outlook and a brighter horizon.

If you can't quite see that light, can't quite feel the Savior's strength and comfort, pray for it. It's a gift He wants to give you. For those who put up a brick because there's an unwanted distance to the Savior, the only way to destroy this brick is to destroy whatever blocks you from Christ. If it's sin, pray for a change of heart, the ability to turn your heart to Christ and to commit yourself to obedience one prayer, one commandment, one step at a time—never on your own, always with Him.

Satan is a master brick builder. He'll work right alongside us, helping, hewing, hoisting until we've built a wall that will keep us away from a joyful life and trapped on the loathsome side of misery where he dwells. He does this by convincing us that no matter how hard we try, we are not good enough— that in God's eyes, we'll *never* be good enough. That's a lie!

Exaltation is not something we earn. After all we can do, we'll never do enough. It's a gift granted to us *after all* we can do by *His grace* (see 2 Nephi 25:23).

Don't let that discourage you. What you do matters. Every effort you make makes a difference. Don't give up. That wall will come down if you keep working in tandem with the One who knows just where and how to bring it down.

Other Bricks to Consider

While every brick wall is different, there are some bricks that most of us have in common. We've addressed emotions over and over because emotions drive our lives. But remember, we are not our feelings. Understanding that and learning how to separate our feelings from the facts give us tools to break bricks, especially the emotion ones.

Fear. What makes us afraid? Who told us to fear something in the first place? We have to understand our emotions before we can conquer them. Emotions are something we *feel*—they are not something we *are*. Fear is Satan's favorite emotion. He uses it to crank us in the direction he desires that we go—always downward, always to the edge of death.

The Lord guides with love and trust and freedom. He allows us to think for ourselves and choose for ourselves, and He stays as close to us as we allow Him. Jesus wants to be there for us no matter the circumstances. He's not afraid of the dark.

The only way to remove fear is to face it. Fear will continue to terrify you until the moment you approach it, unmask it, and realize the monster is only as scary as the power you give it. Once you take the power back, the monster shrinks to nothing.

Regret. What a waste of time. If you've done something you shouldn't have done, something that has brought sorrow into your life, repent of it and move on. Wallowing in regret wastes the opportunities you have to do good for yourself and others. Any brick labeled *regret* can be removed through fast and furious repentance and a face to the future, not the past.

Maybe part of breaking that brick down is to make restitution wherever possible. If you've hurt someone, try to fix the damage. If you can't fix the damage, move forward knowing the Lord is the Master Repairman.

But what if you apologize sincerely to someone and he doesn't forgive you? Then a brick goes up on his wall, not yours.

None of us can change the past, but none of us has to stay there.

I once had a young woman in a class I taught who said her biggest regret in life was not taking advantage of an opportunity she could never get back. She'd been seated next to a man on a long-distance flight. Their conversation had turned to religion, and he'd asked her what she believed. She wanted to tell him. "But then I realized how stupid I'd sound if I said that I believed a boy younger than us had seen God the Father and Jesus Christ and angels and ancient records and all that. So I just smiled and said I believed in God."

Would that girl ever have the chance to testify to that man again?

Probably not.

But today she is serving a mission, testifying to others.

We can't change the past. We can seldom reclaim opportunities we didn't take advantage of, but we can move forward and learn and do better when we know better. Moving on to the next opportunity is the best way to break a brick labeled *regret*.

Disappointment. How many bricks are made from some sort of disappointment? Didn't get the job. Failed to make the team. Someone we trusted let us down. Disappointment is finite. Hope is infinite.

Anyone who ever attempts anything is going to meet with disappointment at some time or another. How we handle disappointment is what will ultimately determine whether we succeed. The secret here is to realize the journey *is* the destination. The moment of victory isn't at the finish line; it's all along the line—start to finish.

Others. In the research, we discovered that whenever there was a brick with someone else's name on it, the wall owner thought someone else was blocking the way to joy. My spouse. My mother. My father. My sibling. My boss. In reality, we make our own bricks, so if there's a brick in your wall with someone else's name on it, you put it there. You gave that person power over you. Take back your power!

Whenever we become more familiar with someone else's faults than our own, the problem is ours.

Wouldn't life be peachy keen if it were easy to grab a brick and chuck it? We can't always do that because when bricks have other people's names on them, moving those people out of our lives isn't that easy. An adage says a mother can't be any happier than her saddest child. So let's say you have a child who is falling away from the principles of the gospel. Let's say that child is even doing harmful things. That child's destructive behavior becomes your brick. After all, how can you be joyful when your child is in trouble?

This is a tough one. It works the same for anyone you love but especially for those closest to you. When they are miserable, it's easy for you to fall prey to that same misery. All I can tell you is that Jesus was surrounded by many unhappy, unhealthy people, but He still took care of Himself. He made time to get away from the people who drained Him and be alone with His Father. He managed to love everyone but never be codependent on anyone except His Father.

We can learn a lot from that. I know I'm still learning.

Pain. Pain isn't an emotion, but it can stream into all types of emotions. When we temporarily numb our pain, it hurts worse when we finally feel it again. Pain embraced can lead us to the source of what's really wrong so our wound can be mended. A doctor asks, "Where does it hurt?" for that very reason—to discover the source of the pain and therefore the remedy.

Chronic pain is something I have to live with. Too many old injuries. It's no fun, and some days when my pain is high and my threshold is low, the pain robs me of my day's allotment of joy. Lots of emotions are associated with pain: grumpiness, frustration, disappointment, impatience, even anger.

It doesn't have to be physical pain that builds your brick. It can be mental anguish. Emotional heartache. Pain is pain. And pain is universal. The writer James Baldwin said, "You think your pain and your heartbreak are unprecedented in the history of the world, but then you read. It was books that taught me that the things that tormented me most were the very things that connected me with all the people who were alive, or who had ever been alive."

The philosopher Sophocles knew the best way to break a brick labeled *pain*: "One word frees us of all the weight and pain of life: That word is love."

Loneliness. The reason we feel lonely is because God did not program us to be solitary creatures. The world is only wonderful when we have someone with whom to share it. And trust me, it's possible to feel alone even when you are in the presence of someone else. Unhappily married people are some of the loneliest souls on earth.

You can't change another person, but you can change yourself. You can change your thoughts. You can banish loneliness by becoming best friends with yourself. Be someone who is ever learning and coming to a knowledge of life. Be someone who seeks adventure and experience. Meet new people. Bond more fully with old acquaintances. Once you learn to like you, loneliness will never be a problem again.

Unforgiveness. That's a brick that seems to replicate itself. Once unforgiveness finds a place on our wall, it blocks out all kinds of good things that lead to joy. I don't think it's inherent in mere mortals to readily forgive. We have to work at it. We have to pray for the strength to do it—over and over and over and over. There are always going to be situations that require forgiveness.

Let it go so you can go.

Forgive because the Lord commands it. Understand why the Lord gives such a commandment: because He wants us to be free to join Him on the side of joy.

Forgiveness is not just about saying the words. It's about begging for a portion of the Lord's Spirit to cleanse our hearts and minds of unkindness or bitterness toward those who have hurt or offended us. It's about that same Spirit filling the empty void with light and love.

Forgiving is within our control. It's a choice for us to forgive others. But what if we have a brick in our wall because we need to be forgiven—and we need to *feel* forgiven?

We all know how to repent, but do we know how to accept pardon when it comes? The need to forgive ourselves is a common brick. It is removed only when we can extend mercy to ourselves so the Lord can extend that same Spirit of mercy to us. It comes down to a matter of our self-worth. Do we love ourselves as the Lord has commanded? If not, our prayers might well beg for that ability.

To forgive others, to forgive ourselves, and to seek forgiveness is all part of the brick-breaking plan. Forgiveness prevents Satan from getting an advantage over us (see 2 Corinthians 2:10–11). Never forget that Satan has to find a foothold before he can muster a stronghold.

There will always be reasons for bricks. There are too many to name.

But there will always be help available to you to break them down. Remember, God wants you to live on the other side of that wall.

The Wall

Here's the thing about the wall that stands between you and joy—it's all in your head. It's not real. Yes, the circumstances are real. Your loss is real. Your pain is real. But every single brick, no matter how big, is an obstacle that blocks you only in your thinking.

But sometimes the things in our heads are as real as stone. It was a fact that I couldn't swim, and my inability to swim made me insecure and unhappy. It's also a fact that when I learned to swim, I experienced a kind of joy I couldn't have known before. It's not so much in the swimming as it is in the overcoming.

Albert Schweitzer said it poignantly: "One who gains strength by overcoming obstacles possesses the only strength which can overcome adversity" (in Long Ho, *Unconditional Love: A Love That Lasts* [2014], ebook).

I promise you that as you identify and tear down brick after brick, you can find joy. And you don't have to tear down the whole wall before you can live joyfully in an unhappy world. It begins with that very first brick letting sunlight through where darkness has been.

You can be joyful in spite of facing rejection.

You can be joyful in spite of suffering pain.

You can be joyful for what you have instead of mourning what you don't have.

God stands at the door waiting to help tear down your wall. Satan tried his best to put up a wall for Jesus. Jesus knew pain. He knew betrayal. He knew rejection. People lied about Him. They lied *to* Him. He knew loneliness. He knew sorrow. He witnessed humanity at its worst.

Yet Christ overcame, and that means you and I can overcome too. We can overcome whatever blocks us from the joy that Jesus wants us to experience, for to experience joy is to achieve the truest level of success.

Chapter Six
EXPECT A MIRACLE

"There are only two ways to live your life. One is as
though nothing is a miracle.
The other is as though everything is a miracle."
—Albert Einstein

THERE IS A FUN STORY about a pastor in Romania who wasn't particularly fond of a kitten that made itself at home in the church yard. One day he heard the little kitten mewing frantically. The curious kitten had climbed high in the tree and couldn't get down.

Thinking quickly, the pastor used a rope to tie the thin branches of the tree to the bumper of his car; he figured that if he drove forward slowly and bent the top branches, they'd bow down and the cat could scramble to safety. But the plan went awry when the rope snapped and the wide-eyed kitty was catapulted high into space.

Feeling terrible, the pastor went in search of the cat. Because the neighborhood was so compact, there were alleys, fences, and scraps of yards with hundreds of trees and endless possibilities. Despite the pastor's determined efforts, the kitten was nowhere to be found. He gave up and left the cat's care in the hands of the Creator.

Days later he ran into one of his parishioners in the grocery store. The only item she was purchasing was a bag of cat food.

"I didn't know you had a cat," he said.

"Oh, Pastor, it's a miracle!" she answered. "My little daughter has always wanted a pet, but I said, 'No, unless God brings you one Himself, there's no way.' Then the other day when she was praying, a kitten rained down from heaven, right out of the blue sky and right through her open bedroom window."

The pastor stood silently, his jaw hanging down and his eyes bugged out.

"Oh, I can see that you don't believe me. But I swear it's true. A true miracle!"

All the pastor could do was nod. A miracle indeed!

This cute story illustrates the point that joyful people expect miracles. They pray for miracles. They live like good things are headed their way. They *expect* God to bless them. Hebrews 4:16 teaches us that Heavenly Father is pleased when we come not timidly or ashamed but *boldly* to the throne.

We can expect good from Him because He is good. And *only* good.

Joyful people look for miracles. They *expect* God to bless them. Earlier we discussed how our mind is a door, and we highlighted Christ's example when He approached His lifeless friend, Lazarus.

At the tomb where tradition says Jesus brought Lazarus back to life, there's a spot where you can stop and look back before descending into the dark part of the grave. It's there, where sunlight still filters in, that Jesus supposedly paused to utter a prayer of gratitude *before* the miracle of Lazarus's rising: "And Jesus lifted up His eyes, and said, Father, I thank thee that thou hast heard me. And I knew that thou hearest me always" (John 11:41–42).

What would our lives be like if we prayed with gratitude *before* we received the desired blessing? What would it be like to possess that kind of faith? Go back in your mind to your imaginary brick wall. If all you can manage is to wiggle one brick loose, just enough to let a ray of light shine through, then break it down from there. Believe that the God of light and joy is your champion.

Maybe we wouldn't pray for raining cats, but we could say something like, "Dear Father, thanks for keeping me safe today. Thanks for helping me get the promotion at work. Thanks for keeping my family on the track to joy." We can pray all of these things *before* they happen. That's how we demonstrate not just our faith but also our love and trust.

I love that Jesus thanked His Heavenly Father first. It stands to reason that people with this kind of sure faith are the most joyful. However, that doesn't mean what you might assume.

When little children pray to find a lost item, they pray with faith that when they rise from their knees they will be led to find the item. Somewhere along the passage of time, that sure, pure faith deteriorates. We begin to tell ourselves that *maybe* we won't find our lost toy. Maybe it's God's will that it will never be found. We blame ourselves for being stupid and losing it in the first place. A destructive inner dialogue goes on and on until we've talked ourselves out of a miracle headed our way.

I've had prayers that seemed to go unanswered. I've had prayers that seemed to go unheard. In fact, the first prayer I prayed as a child was offered in the most desperate and dire circumstance. I was locked in a basement in a foster home; the lightbulb had been removed so I was buried in pitch darkness, loneliness, and fear. I prayed with all the faith a child in need could muster.

Nothing happened.
Nothing changed.
Or so it seemed.

I certainly didn't get the answer I wanted. But I did get the answer I needed. I just couldn't see that until years had passed. God was with me all along, even though I couldn't see, hear, or feel His presence. Only in hindsight did I realize He always had my best interest at heart. Often it takes time to allow for a clear perspective. And time takes faith. Faith takes prayer. And prayer takes hope. As long as we keep that cycle going, we can live in joy, knowing we are never alone and never abandoned.

The trick to joy in regard to faith is to keep that childlike expectation alive. Expect miracles. If you want a kitten and pray for a kitten, be warned; it just might start raining cats!

Eyes to See

When asked if they had ever witnessed a miracle, fewer than half of an audience of hundreds of people indicated that they had. The other half shook their heads no. The miracle half believed they led joyful, purposeful lives. The other side? Not so much.

One grumpy-faced man said, "I've lived eighty years and I've never witnessed a single miracle."

Do you think that's possible—for a man to live eight decades and never witness a miracle? Or is it that "having eyes, see ye not? and having ears, hear ye not? and do ye not remember?" (Mark 8:18).

Miracles abound for those with ears to hear, eyes to see, and a mind that searches for times when the Lord intervened. A miracle is an event that demonstrates awe, something spectacular or small that would not and could not have occurred by natural means. It requires intervention.

If you suppose that your life has been short on miracles, consider the last time you watched a flower blossom, held a newborn baby, held the hand of a dying loved one, or witnessed the return of a lost soul back to the fold? Next time you get cut, pay close attention to the miraculous healing process of your body.

Make it a habit before you go to bed to sneak outside and take a peek the stars. The God who rules the heavens is your Father, and you have access to His love and His power. That's a miracle!

Miracles of the Miraculous Man

If you were asked to list the miracles of Christ, you might start with the first miracle recorded in the Bible (turning water into wine at a wedding in Cana). But wait—go back to the book of Genesis. Turning water into wine was nothing compared to the miracle of growing grapes in the first place: "And out of the ground made the LORD God to grow every tree that is pleasant to the sight, and good for food; the tree of life also in the midst of the garden, and the tree of knowledge of good and evil" (Genesis 2:9).

The next recorded miracle has Jesus healing a royal man's son by His word alone (see John 4:46–54). Jesus was in Cana. The young boy who lay dying was in Capernaum. The father begged Christ to hurry to Capernaum, but Jesus simply told him to return home and promised him that his son would live.

And so it was.

But is that the great miracle—that a dying child was healed? Go to the first chapter in the book of John: "In the beginning was the Word, and the Word was with God, and the Word was God. The same was in the beginning with God. All things were made by him; and without him was not any thing made that was made. In him was life; and the life was the light of men. And the light shineth in darkness; and the darkness comprehended it not" (vs. 1–5).

Jesus healed the blind, but before that He was part of the team that designed the human eye. And the ear. And the tongue. And the brain. And the heart. And the body of flesh and bones and tissues and muscles and sinews and cartilage and skin and systems that house the spirit—a spirit that cannot die.

When we begin to see everything as a miracle, from the rising of the sun to the night's billowing blanket of darkness and everything in between then we become part of those miracles. We realize our very lives are miracles—every breath and every blink. It's easy to live in joy when we live in an abundance of miracles.

If we want more miracles in our lives, perhaps we should pray for eyes to see, ears to hear, and a mind that remembers.

Joyful people remember and recount the miracles of their lives. To be around a truly joyful person is to hear about a continuous tapestry of miracles: "Remember the time this happened or that didn't happen?"

Didn't happen? What does that mean?

Foolishly, we don't credit the Lord with the miracles that keep things from happening. Author Jodi Picoult wrote: "It was possible that a miracle was not something that happened to you, but rather something that didn't" (*The Tenth Circle* [New York: Washington Square Press, 2006], 160).

If you ask God to bless you at the beginning of the day and you are safe and sound at the end of the day, how many miracles do you suppose occurred during the day to answer that prayer? A ladder didn't fall on your head. A car didn't careen out of control and crash into you. Your heart didn't stop beating. A maniac didn't shoot you.

It's definitely something to consider and another reason to be grateful and joyful!

Joyful People Rejoice Regardless

Miracles don't always save us from suffering, but when we focus on the power of God, on the magic and miracles of life, we begin to see and feel the synchronicity of life. The more aware we are, the more miracles we receive, even when life doesn't seem quite so miraculous.

Greg was a man not yet sixty years old. He had a lot of life still to live. But the doctor told him that wasn't likely. Greg had stage-four cancer in his head and neck. His prognosis was a few months at best, so his family started planning his funeral.

While his family planned his funeral, Greg slipped out the back door and went on a walk through the countryside with his dog. They strayed from their normal path and ended up at a small, abandoned church in the Georgia pines. Greg sat on the steps and prayed for a miracle.

When he opened his eyes, God showed him the disrepair of the building. Greg's thoughts turned from his own problems to the problems of that sacred building that had served so faithfully but that now stood scarred and neglected.

A feeling entered Greg's heart. A thought came into his mind. He contacted the historical society and asked permission to help repair that church. Three years later Greg was still working on that building, his cancer in remission.

Not all stories end on such a sweet note. All petitions don't get such a joyful response. But that doesn't mean we can't marvel at the miracles around us. That we can't be grateful for what we have, determined to do what we can. That doesn't mean the Lord doesn't love us and doesn't bless us. Sometimes the miracle is simply the strength and courage to get us through the trial and to retain our faith in the face of adversity.

The Greatest of God's Miracles

There are detailed lists of Christ's miracles, but what's the greatest miracle in your personal life? Life itself? Or the ability to transform from one life to the next—to transcend from a lower life to a higher life and to continue to change, always becoming better?

That's the miracle of evolution—the evolving of ourselves.

Progress toward perfection—isn't the power of the Atonement possible only because "God so loved the world, that he gave his only begotten Son, that whosoever believeth in him should not perish, but have everlasting life" (John 3:16)?

The Atonement is the greatest news of all to those who are joyful. Why? Because it's a promise of hope, and without hope, there is no happiness. Why? Because there is no possibility for change. And change is what this gospel is all about.

Joyful People Attract Joyful People

You are a child of God. By that divine connection you are entitled to dream and to achieve those dreams. Help is yours for the having. Don't surrender your joy to those who would limit you. Don't surrender your joy to your own inability to see the miracles that abound in your life.

People who believe in miracles are simply more joyful. It's a statistical fact. In a culmination of surveys and studies conducted over the past decade, believers are a third more likely to express optimism. Nearly half consider their lives "very happy." Of those who consider themselves nonbelievers, half feel like they are failures and their lives are failures. They tend to be gloomier in general.

One-third of the people who believe in life after death are happier than those who don't (see Daniel Petersen, *Deseret News*, Thursday, March 8, 2012).

It all makes perfect sense. People who believe there is unseen help available to them, that there is a God watching over them, that life doesn't end at the grave, and that love lives on are happier than those who find no eternal purpose in any of those things.

I asked the happiest man I know why he's so happy. He said, "Because I keep an eternal perspective."

That means miracles have not ceased!

Moroni asked, "Wherefore, my beloved brethren, have miracles ceased because Christ hath ascended into heaven? . . . Has the day of miracles ceased?" (Moroni 7:27, 35).

No, they have not!

You are the miracle. Imagine that you are Christ's work in progress. You radiate an inner light. You are deeply and authentically good and getting better. You have ears to hear and you take time to listen. You move through life with a sense of inherent value because you know your divine identity. You don't hesitate to laugh, a lot, out loud. You smile at strangers. Your days are infused with gratitude because you are aware of all that you have for which to be grateful. You dwell on God's goodness and not your own. Your spirit is generous, your words true and kind. You are honest as the day is long. You see life as a mortal adventure; you see yourself as an explorer of mortality, a messenger from God to those children who are unable to see themselves for who they are. You produce more than you consume. Your life has balance. Your relationships are priorities. Time is not spent; it's invested. You are a moral character through and through. You are a joyful soul because at this point, there is no other way to be.

Yes, the greatest of all miracles is the miracle of your becoming whom God knows you are meant to one day be.

A Dry, Dead Piece of Wood

There is a beautiful story in the book of Numbers. The children of Israel were at it again. Murmuring. Jousting for position. Living lives that were the polar opposite of joy. The Lord wanted it to stop. He wanted the people to know that Aaron possessed the authority to do what he had been called to do. Can't you just hear the weariness in a parent's voice when God said, "I will make to cease from me the murmurings of the children of Israel" (Numbers 17:5)?

God had Moses gather twelve rods—walking sticks, staffs, shepherds' crooks; whatever they were, they amounted to little more than dry, carved pieces of dead wood. These Moses gathered from the princes of the twelve tribes. Upon each stick, a man's name was written. Aaron's name was written on the rod of Levi.

The rods were then placed in the tabernacle of the congregation, with the Lord's promise that He would settle the dispute by making the rod of His chosen tribe and leader to sprout.

Sure, sure, the children of Israel murmured. They doubted that God could make a dead piece of wood sprout new life. They doubted even after they'd seen His holy hand quell their rebels. They doubted even after all of the miracles they'd witnessed. They doubted in spite of their blessings. They might as well have been called the "children of doubt."

The rods went into what amounted to a special tent.

The rod that sprouted life would indicate who was to be high priest. The Hebrew word for "rod" is *mattah*. It means two things: tribe and chastisement. How appropriate is that? How fitting in this case, since it was the tribe of Levi that was attached to Aaron. I use the word *attached* because even though Levi was one of Jacob's less obedient sons, his name means *attached* in Hebrew.

Those of us who attach ourselves to God are favored of God.

Now those twelve dead pieces of wood, severed from their source of life, were stored away. The children of Israel knew Jesus had been referred to as the vine, and when a branch was severed from the vine, it withered and died—exactly what had happened to all of those pieces of wood.

Only one of them was still symbolically *attached* to God.

Only one of them sprouted not only buds and leaves but even almonds!

This confirmed Aaron as the high priest—God's clear choice (see Numbers 17:1–8).

This story is important for us to remember because it reminds us of God's power in our lifeless, dry, dead, joyless lives.

God can take what is old and dead and make it alive. He can make it fruitful in abundance. God can do miracles with our tired, dry selves if we will lie down before His tabernacle and allow Him to work a miracle.

We can have the life we want, the life we deserve.

A joyful life in an unhappy world is a great and mighty miracle. It's possible, not because we pursue joy in and of itself—beginning with thoughts and ending with thoughts only of ourselves—but because we don't strive to be better than someone else. We strive only to be better than we used to be.

God has made that possible through an Atonement that is uninterrupted. We have power and access to change when we are sincere about becoming better.

And that is joy at its finest.

Chapter Seven

FROM THE INSIDE OUT

"It is not the mountain we conquer, but ourselves."
—Sir Edmund Hillary (Quoted in John Mason,
Know Your Limits—Then Ignore Them
[Tulsa OK: Insight Publishing Group, 1999], 27)

JOYFUL PEOPLE ARE HAPPY FROM the inside out. They know who they are. They know what they're worth. They don't buy into the world's lies. They stay true to the truth that whispers to them from the lining of their souls.

No matter their circumstances, they are free. The Savior declared, "I call heaven and earth to record this day against you, that I have set before you life and death, blessing and cursing: therefore choose life, that both thou and thy seed may live" (Deuteronomy 30:19).

Joyful people choose life. They choose to think for themselves. They choose their own attitudes. They don't let anything or anyone rob them of the greatest gift that God has given us next to life itself—agency.

Circumstance doesn't determine their level of joy—choice does. Joyful people conscientiously choose to participate in the creation of their own lives. They make things happen and don't wait to see what happens to them. They say yes to opportunities. They say no to the things that would hamper their joy.

I have the privilege of working with homeless youth. At a recent meeting, one young man expressed his innermost feelings: "Someone looking at my life from the outside would think that I'm totally messed up. But on the inside I feel nothing but peace and joy because I'm finally free. I'm free from the poison environment where I used to live. I'm free of thinking other people's poisonous thoughts. I'm free to be the person I'm meant to be."

That's why Jesus came—to set us free from sin, be it our own choices or the suffering we endure because of someone else's sin imposed on us. We are free to think for ourselves, to act for ourselves. Christ conquered the ultimate enemy, the foe no one before Him had conquered—death. We tend to forget that He not only overcame physical death but that His Atonement also freed us from spiritual death. It can set us free when our own thoughts steal our joy, when our own actions prevent us from fully living.

President Thomas S. Monson has talked about the remarkable strides man has made in conquering outer space, but how futile our efforts have been in conquering the inner space of our own hearts and minds (see "In Quest of the Abundant Life," *Ensign*, March 1988).

Jesus wants to strengthen us from the inside out. Paul wrote to the Ephesians, "He would grant you, according to the riches of his glory, to be strengthened with might by his Spirit in the inner man; That Christ may dwell in your hearts by faith; that ye, being rooted and grounded in love, May be able to comprehend with all saints what is the breadth, and length, and depth, and height; And to know the love of Christ, which passeth knowledge, that ye might be filled with all the fulness of God" (Ephesians 3:16–19).

Filled with the goodness of God.

That's a joyful life if ever there was one. Let's break it down into four parts.

Peace to the Mind

When Oliver Cowdery was working alongside the Prophet Joseph Smith, he had his assurances, but Oliver also struggled with doubts. It's okay to have doubts. But don't let your doubts douse your faith. Doubt will do it if you dwell on what you doubt instead of concentrating on what you believe.

Doubts can be directors if we ask God to guide our doubts.

Doubts are what led Joseph Smith into the Sacred Grove. Doubts are what led Spencer W. Kimball to pray for an enlightening revelation on the priesthood. Through Joseph Smith, the Lord revealed the sixth section of the Doctrine and Covenants to quell Oliver's doubts and to bolster his faith: "There is none else save God that knowest thy thoughts and the intents of thy heart" (v. 16).

Isn't that comforting? God is the *only one* who knows your thoughts and intents. We can hide nothing from Him.

Hold up. Does that mean I don't even realize my own thoughts and intents? I think it does. We have an inner critic. We have self-doubts. We often work from confusion and end up startled at our own behavior. "I didn't mean to do what I just did. I had no idea that was going to come out of my mouth. I wasn't thinking."

God knows us better than we know ourselves. That's peace to my mind. Through Him I can come to know myself and my own true worth. That's what joyful people realize and do.

To Oliver, the Lord asked, "Did I not speak peace to your mind concerning the matter? What greater witness can you have than from God?" (v. 23).

Oliver, working with Joseph, had doubts about his own mission and the work he was to do. This answer brings peace to all of us who wonder the same thing: "Whoso desireth to reap, let him thrust in his sickle with his might, and reap while the day lasts, that he may treasure up for his soul everlasting salvation in the kingdom of God" (v. 3).

Joseph Smith is a stellar example of this principle. If we want to live joyfully, our minds must be filled with peace, even when facing the most horrendous circumstances. Joseph had developed a fabulous vision of leading the Saints to the safe haven of the Rocky Mountains. It was right up there at the top of his bucket list. He pictured himself as Moses, shepherding those he loved across the plains to a place where they could not be driven out or burned out. In the shadow of the great Rockies, Joseph's Saints would be safe at last.

But as the furor against him grew, Joseph realized that dream was not going to materialize—not for him, anyway. He had to give it up and instead accept the mission before him. He had to surrender to a court of supposed justice. It was his inner peace that kept him joyful and strong. It was his love for his God, himself, and his fellowman that gave Joseph the strength to admit, "I am going like a lamb to the slaughter; but I am calm as a summer's morning; I have a conscience void of offense towards God, and towards all men" (D&C 135:4).

Joseph taught us that inner peace *is* strength. Joyful people simply do good when faced with bad. They do good when and how they can. They don't question; they just do. Joyful people trust their own desires to do good. They don't go around muttering, "Am I good enough?" They just do it, knowing God makes all the difference as long as we give what we can and do what we're able. Joyful people then work from an inner sense of peace that even if they do make a mistake, it's going to be okay in the end because God is in charge.

Strengthened by His Spirit

Joyful people don't rely on their own strength. They rely on God's infinite strength and abilities. They don't have to fear that they're marching alone because they know they're not. They work and walk in tandem, strengthened by His spirit.

Perhaps the best and fastest way to be joyful is to release all the things that make you sad. Yet it's not that easy because we timidly and fearfully cling tight to whatever is comfortable and familiar.

But there is a difference between being comfortable and being comforted.

Think of the cildren of Israel wandering through the desert for forty years, circling the same mountain, eating the same manna, and wearing the same shoes. No kidding. The same shoes! (See Deuteronomy 29:5.)

I don't know about you, but I'd get mighty bored and maybe even severely depressed with a life that was comfortable but that did not include the comfort and joy that comes with a new pair of shoes or the taste of a new recipe or an adventure to a place I'd never been.

Did you know that their forty-year trek could have been made in eleven days? Walking the most direct route from Horeb by way of Mount Seir to Kadesh Barnea can be done in eleven days (see Deuteronomy 1:2). When eleven days turns into forty years, you know you've got a problem.

What more could God have given the children of Israel? They had a living prophet among them. Those former slaves had literal access to Moses. Even though there were millions of them, they had the ability to feel of his spirit, to seek wisdom from his inspired mind, to see him and hear him.

The Lord had delivered them from their Egyptian captors. So the children of Israel knew they were free. They knew God loved them. They knew God's power was on their side. After all, they'd participated in the parting of the Red Sea. They'd seen what happened to those God did not favor.

Shouldn't that have been enough to bring them great joy?

When they were thirsty, God made water spring forth from a rock.

When they were hungry, He gave them manna to nourish and sustain them.

But was that enough? Nope. They murmured. They whined. They disobeyed.

When they were confused, He called their prophet to the top of a mountain so He could give them instructions—personal directions on how to live joyfully and triumphantly. But while Moses was away, oh, how the children did play.

They pulled out their idols and threw a party for a god who had never blessed them.

Was it any wonder, then, that God let them wander, lost and comfortable but not comforted? Was it any wonder that only a few of the original numbers ever made it across the border into Cana? Most of them died "comfortably" in the wilderness without ever laying foot in the promised land.

Special Resources

If you were locked away in a tower for years with no human contact, only food and water reeled up to you on a pulley, how would you entertain and care for yourself? Joyful people have special resources in their own minds to call on when they need wisdom and guidance and when they need consoling.

For starters, joyful people laugh. They laugh at thoughts in their own heads. They laugh at memories. They laugh at the humor in the world around them. There is a Yiddish proverb that says, "What soap is to the body, laughter is to the soul." One thing that really keeps me positive and up and going is having a sense of humor. There are a lot of things I find really funny, and I believe that seeing the humor in things can dramatically change your life. When I see people around me laughing and smiling, and when I see joy and love around me, I am reminded of everything I love about life.

Learning is ongoing for joyful people. They never tire from mastering new skills. "What did you learn today?" you ask a joyful soul. The answers might surprise you. "Today I learned that *khoda hafez* is how to say 'goodbye' in Farsi." Or "I learned that in Lucerne, Switzerland, you can hire an evil-looking clown to stalk your child for a week before her birthday, then for no added charge, the clown will smash a cake in your child's face on the special day."

They also learn poetry and scripture to recall when they need a friend. Poems and scriptures are friends, you know— loyal and ready friends. The truth is that joyful people are humble people, always willing to learn something new and ready to master a new skill.

As for memorizing scriptures, your mind can bring to light God's word in your darkest times. When your destructive self-dialogue says you can't, you can counter, "I can do all things through Christ [who strengthens] me" (Philippians 4:13).

Joyful people are good and kind and true no matter who is or is not watching. They maintain their integrity and don't have to live in fear or shame.

Joyful people share their fruit. The Bible doesn't say whether Aaron shared the almonds that grew from his staff when the Lord chose him to be Israel's spiritual leader, but the Lord does want us to share our fruits. I have a neighbor who gets more out of sharing the bounties of her garden than she gets out of the gardening itself. "It's my joy," she says every year when she blesses our family with cucumbers and tomatoes.

Joyful people tell stories. They remember good times, sad times, and funny times, and they relate those stories to life. One of the things that brings joy to my life is looking at photographs of my children and recalling the stories that accompany those pictures. I see how far they've come, ever growing, ever learning, sometimes faltering and falling, giving us more stories to share and lessons to apply.

Joyful people are creative. They don't just think outside the box; they destroy the box. They use whatever resources are available to get the job done. Whether you realize it or not, you have a gift to be a creator. You might restore old cars, bake tasty cakes, mow a lawn with precision, fly an airplane, or have a knack for rocking a baby to sleep. Look for things you can do that nurture the creative side of you, and you'll find yourself joyful.

Gratitude is the sense that fills a joyful person's heart. Gratitude builds up a sort of psychological immune system that can cushion us when life knocks us down. Joyful people consciously and consistently look for their blessings, and in the looking, they find their joy.

Joyful people keep an eternal perspective. *This too will pass*, be it pleasant or painful. The things we do now matter later. No effort is wasted.

And joyful people live beyond themselves. They live to make others happy as well as themselves.

Joyful people live freely. They aren't burdened by unnecessary debt, fear, or guilt. They've been frugal and prudent and penitent. When negative feelings do surface—things like anger, fear, envy, or remorse—they see them for what they are: warning signs that something is wrong and needs to be fixed.

Christ Lives on the Inside

One of the most potent scriptures was penned by Paul, who knew what a change of heart meant, what a 180-degree change of life meant. "Christ liveth in me: and the life which I now live in the flesh I live by the faith of the Son of God, who loved me, and gave himself for me" (Galatians 2:20).

Did you know that before Paul was a prophet of God he was an enemy to God? He used to stand at the temple in Jerusalem and mock and belittle Peter and the others who claimed to know and follow Christ. He held the coats of those who stoned Stephen to death. Paul knew about true and eternal change and the joy a changed life can bring.

I promise you that no matter how far down the wrong road you are, Christ will help you turn around and change. Don't let Satan or any voice that speaks for him tell you otherwise. You can live joyfully. Yes, you!

When Christ lives in us, our lives are no longer lived for selfish reasons. We see people for who they are in God's eyes, and we recognize that everyone has infinite worth.

We Christians talk a great deal about going "out." Out of Egypt. Out of the wilderness. Out of bounds. Out of control. But maybe we should talk more about coming "in." The eleven-day journey that took forty years was the time it took to prepare the children of God to enter *into* the promised land. That's a lifetime. Joshua and Caleb were the only adults older than twenty from that first generation who were allowed to enter. Why? Because when they came back from spying on their enemies, they didn't say, "Oh, no! We can't do this!"

They had faith. Faith in God and in their own abilities. Their report was positive and hopeful.

It's one thing to follow the Lord as He leads us out of spiritual death and sin and guilt. He's our rescuer, then, and we're overjoyed to follow Him "out," where our sins are forgiven and our burdens lifted. Hallelujah!

It's quite another thing to follow Him into the promised land. A new life in Christ. An exalted way of living. A foreign land. Because it's not easy, we balk. Because it's not familiar, we murmur. For a journey to be complete, we have to cross over—all the way over to where we can live in spiritual victory.

Not many of us make it. We want the leadership, we want to comfort, but we don't really want a complete "relocation." A new citizenship. A new identity.

Rejoice in the fact that our God is a faithful God. His patience is infinite. He has brought us *out* in order to bring us *in*.

So all the outside work people do to appear happy is just that—an appearance. The Lord wants our joy to emanate from within. Maybe someone looking at my life from the outside would see all the flaws and struggles and assume that my life isn't joyful.

How wrong they'd be. Because true joy starts from the inside and works its way out. President David O. McKay taught that "a martyr at the stake may have happiness that a king on his throne might envy" (Conference Report, Oct. 1955, 4–9).

I think I know what he meant by that.

Chapter Eight
ONE DIRECTION

"When I let go of what I am, I become what I might be."
— Lao Tzu

MY TEENAGE HOBBY WAS RAISING rabbits. They were soft and quiet and so cute. I started out with four bunnies and ended up with more than ten times that many. My grandfather built a sturdy pen for them that featured many individual compartments. But those bunnies seemed so unhappy in their little individual stalls that I got the bright idea to make one giant pen and let them all live together. I found a nice open area with lots of leafy greens, dirt, and rocks. I dug as deep as I could around a circular perimeter and planted chicken wire so they couldn't dig underneath and escape. Then I poured buckets of bunnies into the circles, put out watering dishes and pellet dispensers, and off I went, happy that I had made my rabbit family so happy.

When I checked on them the next morning, I was devastated to find they were all missing. All nine million of them. Scattered over a hundred acres of growing green lucerne.

I'm not sure what happened, but I learned that bunnies can dig deeper than I dug. In all my planning to keep the bunnies inside the pen, I failed to protect them from what might enter the pen. A dog. A cat. A fox. I'm not sure what animal jumped over my wire, but in the act, the animal laid it level and made an open pathway through which the panicked rabbits ran.

So began my rescue operation. I chased rabbits for days. Among the many lessons I learned from that experience is that it's impossible to chase more than one rabbit at a time. If you do, they all escape.

It's the principle the Lord taught when He declared, "No man can serve two masters: for either he will hate the one, and love the other; or else he will hold to the one, and despise the other. Ye cannot serve God and mammon" (Matthew 6:24).

Truly joyful people pursue one main purpose. They serve a single master. They are able to focus and move forward in one direction—forward.

Your Life Has Always Had Purpose

The great plan of happiness testifies to us that our lives have always had purpose. How we pursue that purpose varies greatly. Heavenly Father has prepared not only a plan but also an individual purpose to your existence. Your eternal existence. When questioned, most people don't understand why they exist. Why they're on this earth at this time. We know it's because God wants all of His children to progress and to become like Him. Our time, right here, right now, provides opportunities for that progression. There is no other way.

We came to receive a physical body that could experience both joy and pain. A body that could feel and do. That could tempt us. A mind that could think and choose freely. We were granted agency that we might choose between good and evil. We are here to learn. To experience the widest array of experiences. Brigham Young taught that no experience is wasted as long as we learn something from it. We are also here to bond with other human beings who are on the journey of mortality with us. We are to form family and relationships and friendships, knowing they have the potential to become eternal.

An eternal perspective assures us that when this life is over, life does not end. We can return to live with Heavenly Father and our loved ones. We can continue our journey of moving forward.

All of us, at one time or another, question our purpose for existing. It's easy to seem small and even inconsequential in the grand scheme of life. No life is inconsequential. I love to teach people that Heavenly Father's perfect plan would not be perfect without *them*! Every life matters. Every life has meaning and purpose.

Guess what? You get to choose what that purpose is. As I pointed out at the beginning of this book, Lehi taught his son Jacob, "Man is that he might have joy." That means God's intent is for you to have joy. Whether you accept that gift is up to you. You are free to choose which path you take.

Jesus Christ is the Prime Exemplar. "I have given you an example, that ye should do as I have done to you" (John 13:15).

We *should* do as He did. Still, the choice is up to us.

We might squirm at this scripture because Jesus was the divine exception. He came to earth knowing His purpose. He came to earth as half-God. You are I are 100 percent mortal.

Our ultimate purpose is the same as His—we exist to choose whether we will live joyfully. We've established that living joyfully means living for the things that will bring us closer to God and make us more like Him. We want to live in an eternal state of growth and progress and advancement.

We've gone over different ways that joy can be obtained, but in the end, it all comes down to whether we are pursuing the purpose of our existence. An adage states that the purpose of life is a life of purpose.

Have you decided what your purpose is? Are you actively seeking to fulfill that purpose? When confronted by Pilate, Jesus said, "To this end was I born, and for this cause came I into the world, that I should bear witness unto the truth" (John 18:37).

Did Jesus bear witness to the truth?

How about us?

What is our truth? Jesus is (see John 14:6). Have we born witness of Jesus? Do our lives reflect His will?

"I don't even know where to start," a returned missionary confessed. "Up until now my life has been structured for me. From this point on, I'm supposed to figure out my purpose and go after it. But I'm stuck. I want to serve the Lord, but how do I know which path I'm supposed to take?"

The Lord seldom cares if you become a dentist or a hair designer. He cares if you live a joyful, obedient, full life. Yes, you have certain aptitudes and abilities, and we all need guidance on how to flesh those out to see if they can lead us to a career, a purpose, a direction that will bring us joy. This is the stage in life, and it doesn't matter how far down the line you are or aren't when you decide to pursue your purpose—when you become your own creator. You get to choose what you think will make your life joyful and fulfilled. And you get to choose again if your initial path doesn't lead where you thought it would.

Isn't that spectacular news? You get do-overs. But you don't get more time, so choose as wisely and prayerfully as possible. Know what you want your life to look like, to be like. Picture it. Know the price you are going to have to pay to obtain that life.

Don't get trapped into thinking joy is something that can be held in your hand or accounted for in your bank. It's a gift that comes to you as you live your life fully and faithfully.

Yes, but what about right here and now—the practical things?

Does your career have to align with your divine purpose?

That's a question only you can answer, but it's certainly one you should consider, especially when 80 percent of the American population hate their jobs. It just makes sense that we'll be more effective in our careers if the work we do lines up with the purpose we feel.

What if you want to be a chef? How can that line up with your purpose for testifying of truth?

Where does the food come from? Why are there so many flavors and textures and colors? How can a chef teach about a God who loves variety? How can a chef teach about nutrition and the miracle of the human body and its taste buds? The possibilities are endless.

A chef is more than a person who prepares food. We fill many roles. Every role we play is an opportunity for us to pursue our purpose—not by words, but by the way we live.

I know a man who served as a stake president for many years. The week following his release he was called to serve in his ward's nursery. People expected him to be hurt or offended. Instead, he was joyful, grateful for a change of pace and a new opportunity to learn and grow and gain experience.

His example ignited his entire stake in a way it hadn't while he was serving behind a pulpit.

There is a woman who was born with a gift for healing. Does the Lord care if she becomes a doctor, a nurse, a dentist, or a therapist? As long as she is true to her gift, the Holy Ghost let her know that any career is acceptable to Heavenly Father.

Is a neurosurgeon more valuable in God's eyes than a man who changes automobile tires? Absolutely not. The point is that our individual purpose is found through the process of self-discovery. It's a path few dare venture down. It's a path that demands to know what you truly believe, how deep your commitments go, what makes you joyful, and what steals your joy.

It's often in random, unexpected moments that the Spirit will reveal direction and knowledge about your purpose. Learn to listen to and cherish those arbitrary moments of understanding.

As spirit children of Heavenly Father, we received our primary understanding and lessons "in the world of spirits and were prepared to come forth" on the earth (D&C 138:56). Now we're here, and our Savior wants us to wake up every morning with a definite purpose in our hearts and in our lives.

It's time. It's time for you to let go of everything that stands between you and a joyful life, one where *nothing* stands between you and Jesus.

Are You Aware of Your Passion?

Years ago, a young man on the cusp of his career choices visited Canada. He saw something he had not seen in the United States—submarine sandwich shops. When he went home, he asked his grandfather for a loan to open a submarine sandwich shop in his neighborhood.

"Look, son, I could loan you the money, but I'm not going to because you need to find something to do with your life that brings 'magic' to your work. When you find that, come back."

The young man was disappointed and even angry at first, but when he thought about it, he realized he had always wanted to make movies. So he went back to ask his grandfather for money to buy a movie camera.

Today that man is one of Hollywood's most honored directors.

The happiest people in the world are those whose internal drives align their passion with purpose. Passion is the fire inside that keeps you energized. It keeps you awake all night, thinking and planning. You might be an engineer, a heart surgeon, a chef, a hair designer, a personal trainer, a teacher, an auto mechanic; as long as you're passionate about what you do, your job will bring you joy.

But we can't all work in the careers we'd like. Sometimes life takes that option from us. I have always wanted to be a writer. It's my passion, but along the way I've had to supplement my income by working for a veterinarian; laboring in a slaughterhouse (that job didn't last a full day), an assembly-line factory, an engineering firm, a computer software company, and a pet store; and doing sales jobs, teaching jobs, counseling work, and just plain old grunt work.

That's okay.

Every one of those experiences taught me something about myself and what I really want out of life. They've attuned me to my intuitive powers. Opened my truest desires. Regardless of external judgments and opinions, I've come to know my own purpose and how it aligns with Heavenly Father's will.

Here are a few fun little facts to make you smile. Oprah Winfrey used to bag groceries. Brad Pitt donned a chicken suit and stood on a Los Angeles street corner to sell chicken wings. Beyoncé worked sweeping up hair in her mother's hair salon. Madonna was a waitress at Dunkin' Donuts. Gwen Stefani mopped floors at Dairy Queen. Jennifer Lopez was a file clerk.

The point is that every step is a step to somewhere else. It's called progress, and it's what the Lord wants us to be making.

Do you have a talent you've been afraid to pursue? Or didn't know how to apply? Do you have a gift you're not using but would like to? If you feel that your life needs a shift, a boost, a change, now is the time to start leading the fulfilled, joyful life about which you can be passionate.

Don't be fooled into thinking that in order for you to be successful, you have to make money with your talent. You don't. You can use it for your own pleasure, to bless the lives of others. Money doesn't indicate success. You do. Are you happy doing what you do? Do you make others happy? Are you stretching and developing your gifts? Are you using them for the glory of God?

What if you feel just the opposite—numb? How can you get passionate? You can pray for passion to be a better parent, employee, athlete, intellectual, whatever you'd like to be. As I mentioned earlier, you have the right to go *boldly* to the throne and ask for the help you need to live the kind of life God wants you to live.

Can You See a Pattern to Your Life?

Some people follow a clear path to their purpose. They know from early on what they want to accomplish in their life. Most, though, discover their purpose later on as they become aware of things like patterns. Maybe a few get struck by lightning and that little bubble appears above their heads saying, "This way."

For the majority of us, life is a series of flickering blubs, barely illuminating the way, helping us take steps of faith into the darkness before we reach the light.

Can you look back on your life and see a pattern, a theme of sorts that has repeated itself in your life? What has been predominantly happening in your life, in your thoughts, in your emotions?

Because I wanted to be a writer, I wrote. I wrote all kinds of things. But I didn't find success as a writer until I learned to finish what I started. It's that same concept of chasing after more than one rabbit at a time. Jesus was a master at this principle. Remember, He was administering to someone else when He heard the news about Lazarus. He didn't jump up and run away. He finished His work with the person He was with before He moved on.

Yes, He could be interrupted. Think about the woman with the issue of blood. She touched Him. He stopped moving and interacted with her. When His disciples wanted to protect Him from a throng of needy children, Jesus said, "Suffer the little ones to come unto me."

He had His purpose in mind, His priorities straight, His passion in check. His life was in absolute alignment so He could live in the moment and make the most of the opportunity before Him.

The key is to begin where you are, to know your purpose and understand what is possible, and to trust that God will enable you, if need be, to do the impossible.

Under Divine Obligation

When Howard W. Hunter was President of the Church, he taught that "those of us who have partaken of the Atonement are under divine obligation to bear faithful testimony of the Lord" ("The Atonement and Missionary Work," seminar for new mission presidents, June 21, 1994, 2).

We know from the Savior's example that we are to bear witness of the truth. The truth is that God's perfect plan is in place, and it wouldn't be perfect without each and every one of us.

When the Final Judgment comes and we stand before our Lord and Savior, what do you think He's going to ask about? Not about our careers. Not about our callings. Not about how much money we saved or how many material possessions we accumulated.

He will inquire about those to whom we ministered. Did we soothe the sick, feed the hungry, visit the prisons, and care for the widows and orphans of the world?

Something else He'll ask is how we treated ourselves. Were we kind and forgiving to our own flawed selves? Did we speak kind words? How did we care for the bodies that blessed us through mortality?

When you think about the greatest commandments, it's easy to see whether our lives bear a pattern. Did we do what we were asked and obligated to do? Did we live joyfully no matter how bleak our circumstances?

Joyful

Queen Esther didn't become a queen just so she could wear the crown. Her entire life posed the question to us—"Who knoweth whether thou art come to the kingdom for such a time as this?" (Esther 4:14).

Had she not been where she was, done what did, Esther would not have been in a position to save her people.

We addressed the fact that joyful people expect miracles, but do you ever see your life as a miracle? Have you ever ended up in just the right time and place to help someone in need?

No, we're not Jesus. We're mere mortals. But the message of His final words gives our lives purpose: "Now is my soul troubled; and what shall I say? Father, save me from this hour: but for this cause came I unto this hour" (John 12:27).

HIS life gives our lives meaning. Jesus Christ is the greatest being to be born on this earth. His life is the perfect example of how we should live.

Better Than You Realize

I dare venture that you are doing better at life than you think. Most of us are so busy trying to make something on a grand stage happen that we don't pause to appreciate the little acts that go on behind the scenes.

If you can walk along a beach and feel the joy of warm, wet sand squish between your toes or smell the scent of freshly mowed lawn, if the song of a bird stops you in your tracks and the sight of a shimmering night sky gives you chills, then nature is speaking your language. You are connecting to the source of all joy. You are becoming.

Truman G. Madsen wrote, "'To be or not to be?' That is not the question. What is the question? The question is not one of being, but of becoming. 'To become more or not to become more.' This is the question faced by each intelligence in our universe" (*Eternal Man*, 32).

Joy isn't a goal. Joy isn't a possession. Joy isn't a destination. It's a way of life.

Are you *becoming* more joyful? As we strive to live joyfully, we begin to increase our capacity to be aware of the simple nuances of life. We realize that constant change stirs within us.

Life is never static.

We live in a state of gratitude for what we have; we don't focus on what is lacking. We realize the quality of life we're after isn't based on anything material, but spiritual. It's all about the goodness in our lives, the abundance.

Fifty Facts

Let's look at some of the facts that testify of God's love for you and of His desire for you to live joyfully in troubled times.

1.   You are free to choose how you want to live your life. The fact that you have choices is freedom.

2.   You are walking your own way. I have a Chinese friend who was disowned by her family and community when she joined the Church. Their decisions broke her heart but did not change her mind. "I have to do what's best for me regardless of other people's judgment or opinion," she said.

3.   You are capable of making your own decisions and living with the consequences.

4.   Your hard and smart work invites other people to believe in you and the work you are doing.

5.   You realize that in the end, your life will be a sum of your choices, so you strive to make better choices every day.

6.   You work hard for the people you love and the causes that capture your heart. Someone told me that working hard for something you don't care about is called *stress*. Working hard for something in which you believe is called *passion*.

7.   You, not anyone else, define what joy is for you. You see that it is available in abundance, and you choose to be happy in your own way.

8.   You see the obstacles in front of you as bricks that can be dismantled. You realize you don't have to destroy the entire wall to let joy come shining through. One brick at a time is sufficient.

9.   You see obstacles as opportunities that help you determine that what you believe is worth fighting for.

10. You've survived some tough situations, and you're stronger and wiser and more empathetic as a result.

11. You don't judge. It's not your business.

12. You can look back and see not only how far you've come but also that there has been a continuous pattern to your life, one that leads to the place where your heart aches to go.

13. You don't live in the past. You learn from it and move forward.

14. You are not a quitter. Most people quit by slowing down and slacking off, not in one surprise stop.

15. You accept what you cannot change and realize the only thing you can change is you.

16. You don't see failure in falling down. You see it as experience that leads you forward.

17. Fear does not rule you. Decision does.

18. You have an appreciation for the past, a passion for the present, and a hope for the future.

19. You are always learning and becoming someone stronger, wiser, and better.

20. Your faith wipes out your fear.

21. You realize you're part of a plan and you have a plan. You know what you want.

22. You don't let the opinions or judgments of others stifle your progress or swipe your joy.

23. You are making the most of your resources.

24. You aren't waiting to tackle your bucket list. You're living your dreams now and always adding to that list.

25. You strive to make a contribution. To give more than you take.

26. You're not too timid or too proud to accept the help you need.

27. You consciously look for opportunities to serve others.

28. You love openly and honestly and never fear to express it.

29. You care for your material blessings but don't let them ever mean more than people mean to you.

30. You value and tend to your health.

31. You eliminate the drama from your life by eliminating the people who cause drama.

32. You express your thankfulness but demonstrate your gratitude by giving back to those who can do nothing for you.

33. You seek out adventures.

34. You hone new skills every day.

35. You open your mind to new ideas and to the great thinkers of the world, realizing what Joseph Smith taught: that truth is truth no matter the source.

36. Your word is your bond and you don't speak ill of someone who is not present. If you must speak harshly, you do it privately, gently, and with respect for that person's feelings.

37. You don't allow toxic people to infest you.

38. You realize you are not alone as long as you have God.

39. You like your own company.

40. You recognize the people who have been there for you and you try to be there for others.

41. You express your feelings to the people who have stood with you when you needed them.

42. You travel at every opportunity and create those opportunities yourself.

43. You spend time in the cathedral of nature.

44. You make time for what's most important.

45. You have a home. A house is a home when it shelters the body and comforts the soul. But a home isn't always a physical structure or a specific location on a map. Home is wherever the people you love are, whenever you're with them. It's not a defined place but a space in your heart and mind that builds upon itself like little bricks being stacked to create something stable that you take with you for your entire life, wherever you may go.

46. You realize when to let go and when to hold on. This means you accept rather than resist life's lessons.

47. You recognize that little victories in your life will not only help you find moments of pure joy, but they will help you to live joyfully too.

48. You live with purpose.

49. You do your best to follow Jesus Christ.

50. When you fall down, you reach for His hand to save you.

The Choice Is Yours

Heavenly Father loves you. He's held nothing back from showing that love, including His innocent, unmatched Son. This world, with all its beauties and wonders, exists for your enjoyment and advancement. The horrors that are allowed give you opportunities to learn and grow and understand yourself so you can live a conscious life, one where you think freely and choose freely. One where you evaluate your choices and choose deliberately what speaks truth to you. You understand and appreciate the gift of freedom so you can silence the voices from individuals and society. You tune into your most inner voice, the one that speaks truth to your soul.

Because your mind is a door, you can open it or close it. You can chase out the thoughts that aren't welcome. You realize what you can and should control but that when it comes down to the bare truth, God alone is in control. Knowing that alleviates your need to rush around and your need to try to control people and situations that are not within your power to control.

When bad things happen, you have an inner peace because you rely on God's control, His comfort, and His love. Even though it hurts now, even though life doesn't make sense, your eternal perspective promises that someday it will all make sense.

An old newspaper ad depicts an artist before a canvas. The message says that by changing enough small pictures, we can change the big picture. We know that's true because we understand life is about change. The gospel of Jesus Christ enables change.

Dostoyevsky wrote in his work *The Brothers Karamazov* that "the mystery of human existence lies not in just staying alive, but in finding something to live for" (New York: Farrar, Straus and Giroux; 12th ed., 2002). We exist to experience joy. Anything that stands between us and joy can be removed, one brick at a time. But we don't have to wait until a whole wall is down before we can let joy flow into our lives.

Joyful people forgive quickly. Extend mercy. Show compassion. Why? Because it's innate in them and because they realize *they* need forgiveness, mercy, and compassion. It comes down to living the Golden Rule.

Children of God have the right to expect miracles. We worship a God of miracles. He delights in granting miracles to us as we need them and as we strive to be worthy. Miracles abound. All we have to do is have eyes to recognize the miracles in our lives.

The greatest miracles aren't gigantic feats like parting a sea or restoring sight to the blind. The greatest miracles work from the inside out. They are the cleansing, strengthening, enlightening changes that occur from within us. To change a heart is to change a life, and to change a life is the greatest of all miracles.

As God's child, you are entitled to live a life of purpose. That means your opinion matters. You have the right to do the things that bring you joy, to think and act for yourself. You can overcome your bad habits, the stains of sin, even your very DNA through the atoning blood of Jesus Christ. You don't have to live in shame or guilt. You can live clean and free!

There's a veil, thin and penetrable, between this life and the next. Life is over in a blink, even if you live to be one hundred. Your time on earth isn't about gaining things, it's about growth.

You are the creator and keeper of your joy. Please don't waste a second of your precious time on earth feeling miserable or hopeless. Not when His "hand is stretched out still" (Isaiah 9:21) to embrace you, to invite you to live a joyful life, even though the world around you is troubled.

God will never run out of joy; it's His gift to you for the taking. So go for it. Ask to receive. Speak truth. Dance, even when you look like a fool. Pray always. Sing out loud even if you don't know the lyrics. Expect miracles—great big happy miracles.

Say yes more often. Say no more often. Take chances. Make changes. Risk love. Write old-fashioned letters. Feel the pain so you can release it. Spend money on what makes you better.

Spend time on what makes you happy. Create something. Remember it all, but cling only to the good stuff.

Share all you have. Do good. Do better. Unplug. Hug strangers. Listen with your lips tight and your heart wide open. Learn something new. Obey. Forgive. Move on. Keep dancing, even when you can't hear the music. Make new friends. Don't neglect the old friends. Mourn your losses. Make mistakes—big, brave mistakes.

Celebrate Wednesdays and weekends. Sleep soundly. Share your faith. Dream in color. Kiss the mirror. Laugh until your abs tighten up. Say thanks. Look up. Talk to God and listen for His voice in quiet places. Worship in the cathedral of nature. Look soul-deep into someone's eyes.

See yourself for who you truly are—a child of God of infinite value. Get out there and live! Live! Live! And while you're living, grab all the joy you can.

What are you waiting for?

About the Author

TONI SORENSON WAS IN FOURTH grade when she won her first writing award. *The Salt Lake Tribune* named her an "Aspiring Author." In seventh grade she won top honors as Utah's Young Author in Creative Fiction. In college she was named one of America's most promising writers and the Nashville Songwriters New Song of the Year winner for lyrics she penned.

Her nationally published works have sold more than a half million copies. Her alliance with Covenant Communications has yielded more than twenty published works, including *Master* and *Messiah*, accounts of the life of Christ. Her most recent novel, *Peter*, tells the story of a disciple who dedicated— and gave—his life to Jesus of Nazareth.

Toni won the prestigious Association of Mormon Letters Novel of the Year award for *Redemption Road*. In 2013 Covenant honored Toni with the Making-A-Difference award.

Toni is the mother of six. She spends her time writing, traveling, speaking, hiking, and just "hanging out" with her children, grandchildren, and friends.